Help Me!

Help Me!

A Psychotherapist's Tried-and-True
Techniques for a Happier Relationship
with Yourself and the People You Love

RICHARD B. JOELSON, DSW

HEALTH PSYCHOLOGY PRESS
New York City

Health Psychology Press, New York City
© 2016

Published 2016
Cover design and Book design by Duane Stapp
Printed in the United States of America
Library of Congress Control Number: 2016933752
ISBN 978-0-99722-9202
EBook 978-0-9972292-2-6
10 9 8 7 6 5 4 3 2 1

Dedication

This book is dedicated, with my deepest gratitude, to the hundreds of women, men, and children who chose to place themselves in my care and trusted me to help them successfully address the issues for which they consulted me.

Over the years, I have worked with individuals ranging in age from five to ninety. I have treated people dealing with lifelong emotional difficulties as well as those suffering from the effects of a traumatic experience, like many who came to see me after the events of 9/11. Many patients entered therapy feeling confused and defeated about their experiences and marked by frustration and failure, and left therapy having achieved meaningful growth and change along with renewed hope.

It has always been an honor to have an opportunity to become a meaningful part of each person's life in this unique relationship called psychotherapy. I would like to believe that the vast majority of my patients grew from our association. I thank them all for helping to make me a better therapist and a better person.

Contents

LIVING: Our Relationships with Others

LOVING: Our Partnered Relationships

THRIVING: In All of Our Relationships

Introduction

If someone gave you this book, it is probably because they care about you and want you to enjoy the benefits of one or more of the essays that they themselves found helpful. They may be one of my patients who is familiar with my writing and found some of my ideas useful.

It is always gratifying to hear a patient say "That wasn't boasting, that was pride!" or "I realized that I was only thinking about my situation, but doing nothing at all about it." The patient who said, "For the first time I was just able to quietly listen and not feel compelled to solve her problem" made both of us happy. The patient who learned to distinguish between reacting and responding was able to master the latter and diminish the frequency of the former.

If, because of these essays, you are able to strengthen your thinking, understand something heretofore unclear, or act in a way that represents a personal or interpersonal advance, then I, as a therapist and author, will have accomplished a very meaningful objective.

In my vocation as a psychotherapist, I have had the privilege of being invited into the private lives of hundreds of people seeking help for a great variety of reasons and I have given my best efforts to those who have entrusted me to help them improve their lives. As a result of this work, I have learned a great deal about why some people manage to thrive and succeed while others struggle or fail, why relationships are so difficult for so many and what can be done to make them more successful and fulfilling. I have heard many people describe their lives and their relationships as downhill rides and I have come to understand what can be done to help change that.

This book is a compilation of essays about the social and psychological phenomena that have come up in the course of my efforts to help the people in my care. These individuals and couples have provided me with opportunities to explore and share observations and ideas that have aroused my curiosity and interest throughout my years as a helping professional. "Is dependency unhealthy?" "Why am I shy?" "If there is an us, what happens to me?" and "Am I dating or am I in a relationship?" are just some of the questions I explore.

One of the common laments heard from many people who have sought help is that after much therapy they feel "insight rich and change poor," which is the title of one of my essays. While self-awareness and knowledge increase, this does not necessarily translate into much-needed and desired change. My hope is that you will find some of the essays useful as you look to improve your own personal and interpersonal strengths, internal resources, and overall life experience. Perhaps they will assist you with converting some of your own insights into the changes you have been seeking.

My introduction to the mental health field was somewhat special. I was serving as a Peace Corps volunteer teacher in Liberia, West Africa, and needed a work project while school was out for the summer. My choice was the only mental hospital in the country. There, for several months, I worked with a Canadian psychiatrist and several native healers. The experience dazzled me and I decided to become trained as a mental health professional upon my return to the States after my two-year term of service.

I have enjoyed a diversified professional life throughout my career, both before and after entering private practice. My first job was the proverbial trial by fire. I was given a caseload of one hundred troubled adolescent boys living in a Brooklyn ghetto with a mandate to help keep them out of reform school. After that, I worked as a psychiatric social worker and group therapist in a child and family guidance center. Subsequent employment before full-time private practice included being the Executive Director at a mental health clinic in Greenwich Village, and the Director of Admissions and Student Affairs at the School of Social Work at New York University. I have also taught social work at the bachelor, master, and doctoral level at two New York universities. Currently, I am in full-time private practice in New York City and, after forty-six years, still happy to be doing the work I love.

In this book, I hope to bring all of these experiences together and convey to my readers how strongly I believe in each person's capacity to recover, to grow, to change, and to acquire new abilities and skills at any stage of life.

Richard B. Joelson, DSW, LCSW

Author's Note

I have attempted to organize these essays in a way that will enable you, the reader, to enjoy maximum value from your reading experience. It was not easy!

The categories I've used are Being, Living, Loving, and Thriving. Yet many of the essays could easily be placed in more than one section. Essays about the self have everything to do with how one interacts with others and essays about relationships certainly address issues about the self.

At the end of many essays in this volume, I've included suggestions about others that might elaborate on an idea or further your interest in a particular subject. This book can be read from cover to cover, or you may want to skip to a relevant essay suggested at the end of one you have just completed. The choice is yours. Either way, I hope you find value and enjoyment from what I have offered.

In order to respect and maintain the anonymity of my patients and colleagues, I have changed the names of individuals and places as well as other identifying details.

Being

Our Relationship to Ourselves

EASIER OR BETTER?

*A litmus test for our choices
and decisions...*

Several years ago, I was invited to teach a course in the doctoral program at New York City's Hunter College School of Social Work, where I had earned my doctorate. It was an honor I was eager to accept. The course I was to teach was similar to one that I had taken earlier as a student in the program.

Figuring that I could save a great deal of time and work, I asked the instructor of the course I had taken if I might have a copy of his teaching outline to use for my own class. I said to him, "I think it would be better if I used your outline." His reply was, "No, it wouldn't be better; it would be easier." Somewhat embarrassed by what felt like a mild rebuke from a respected former professor and soon-to-be senior colleague, I thought long and hard about what he had said. Since that exchange, I have put many choices and decisions to the "Easier or better?" test to determine which one I might be using to guide my judgment.

One patient recently provided an excellent example in which she used "better" to replace "easier" in a rather important way. She was having an especially difficult time maintaining her sixth year of sobriety. Her walk home from her Alcoholics Anonymous meeting each week took her past the neighborhood liquor store where she occasionally stopped to "browse the specials in the window." When asked to reflect on this behavior, she joined me in wondering about the obvious risk factors of this route, but claimed it was much more convenient to walk that way (easier) since the alternative route was considerably longer (but better). Fortunately, "better" eventually won out over "easier."

Another patient entered therapy with a rather complex problem. He was scheduled to marry in six weeks, but had become convinced that the marriage was a "disaster in the making," since he was clearly not in love with his fiancée. He had agreed to marry her under pressure, because of their long courtship and because "it seemed like the right thing to do." He asked me for advice, since he was planning to proceed because it was "easier" than suffering the chaos and turmoil of "dropping this bomb" so close to the event. My advice was that we spend some time together sorting this out with the expectation that by doing so, he would not need anyone else's advice but his own. He, too, passed the "Easier or better?" test, realizing that his was a bomb that had to be dropped immediately.

A third patient presented yet another "Easier or better?" issue in a recent treatment session. Believing she was entitled to a raise after four years with no pay increase, she contemplated how to approach her boss and concluded that she would forget about the whole thing. Not asking would be easier than the result she feared: being turned down. Our discussion about what would be best—rather than easiest—for her led to the decision to ask for a raise in salary. She could either celebrate a positive outcome (something she had never contemplated!) or use a negative outcome as an opportunity to strengthen her ability to deal with disappointment and adversity, rather than protect herself by avoiding conflict altogether, as she had done throughout much of her life.

If you think about it, chances are you will recognize examples in your own experience where differentiating between easier and better may help you with an important decision or judgment. The two considerations are often confused, especially given our complex, busy lives, and our wish to accomplish things as quickly and as effortlessly as possible.

THINKING INSTEAD OF DOING

*When intentions become
a substitute for actions...*

Rebecca, a new patient in my psychotherapy practice, was a recent arrival to New York thanks to a company transfer. She was eager to begin dating and indicated an intention to join several Internet dating services to "get the ball rolling" on her social and romantic life in her new city. She also vowed to join two organizations as additional ways of meeting new people, especially men. After several sessions, I noticed that Rebecca had done nothing along these lines, despite her declared eagerness to do everything she said she would and more.

William frequently spoke of his plans to take off twenty-five pounds and begin an exercise program. His motivation was a recent failed stress test and resulting angioplasty, a rather startling development for a heretofore-healthy forty-nine-year-old book publisher. Both Rebecca and William, it turned out, had mixed feelings about acting on some of their good intentions, and so avoided taking the actions necessary to accomplish their goals.

There are many different ways that people manage their anxiety and handle the conflicts that occur in everyday life. Rebecca and William were both demonstrating "thinking instead of doing."

This is a defense against anxiety that involves substituting thought for behavior. The anxiety associated with actual action is kept under control or eliminated altogether. The person who is thinking instead of doing often is soothed and sufficiently reassured so that the actions may become less important than the comfort of believing that action will at some point occur.

Rebecca, for example, was completely convinced that her good intentions and various plans to address her social needs would lead her to take the necessary next steps. In fact, she was so confident and convinced of the eventuality of the required behavior that she sometimes forgot whether or not she had actually acted or just intended to! This suggested the possibility that her intentions may have become a substitute for action (i.e., thinking instead of doing) and that the thinking itself was being experienced as though it had been a behavior. Further exploration revealed that Rebecca harbored terrible fears about whether or not she would ever meet "Mr. Right." In her case, "thinking instead of doing" helped her to avoid the frustrations, worries, and disappointments she had previously experienced and, therefore, associated with future dating. Thinking about dating (while managing not to date) involved the illusion that she was doing something about her social and romantic needs, rather than nothing, which was unacceptable.

William's situation was quite similar. He took great comfort in his good intentions and active thoughts about losing weight and getting in better physical shape, which, of course, was considerably easier and more enjoyable than doing either or both. He, like Rebecca, seemed comfortable not acting on behalf of these important goals. The line between thinking and doing became blurry for William but he was able to recognize how his confidence in the eventuality of his actions almost made the actions themselves seem unnecessary!

If you take a close look at your own intentions, plans, or resolutions for changes you want to make in your life, chances are you will discover at least one area in which your "plan of action" is plan-heavy, but action-light...or without any action at all!

RESILIENCE

Building better coping skills....

If you accept the notion that resilience is something that can be cultivated, as opposed to seeing it only as a genetically determined trait, you might be inspired to strengthen your ability to become more resilient. People often have considerable capacity to build better coping skills, although they are often not sufficiently aware of this.

Resilience is the means by which, for example, children from troubled families are not immobilized by hardship but rebound from it. They learn to protect themselves and emerge as strong adults who are able to lead gratifying lives. The groundbreaking resilience research of sociologist Emmy Werner, PhD, of the University of California at Davis, showed that even during early life about a third of these kids seem to be unaffected by the grinding poverty, alcoholism, and abuse in the homes in which they are raised. Of the remaining two-thirds, many are troubled as teens, typically turning to petty crime. But by the time they reach their 30s and 40s, they have pulled themselves together, determined not to repeat their parents' lives.

A troubled family can indeed inflict considerable harm on its children, but resilient people are challenged by such troubles to experiment and respond actively and creatively. Their preemptive responses to adversity, repeated over time, become incorporated into their inner selves as lasting strengths.

Here are some of the ways that you can build up your capacity to rise above adversity and forge lasting strengths in the struggle. Like so much else in life, these recommendations may be easier said than done. Nonetheless, it is always wise to tap in to your resources and attempt to enhance your self-esteem by being vigorous in efforts to improve yourself.

Learn from your experiences. Recall how you have coped with hardships in the past, either in healthy or unhealthy ways. Build on what helped you through those rough times and don't repeat actions that didn't help.

Remain hopeful and optimistic. While you can't change events, look toward the future, even if it's just a glimmer of how things might improve. Find something in each day that signals a change for the better. Expect good results.

Accept and anticipate change. Be flexible. Try not to be so rigid that even minor changes upset you or that you become anxious in the face of uncertainty. Expecting changes to occur makes it easier to adapt to them, tolerate them, and even welcome them.

Work toward goals. Do something every day that gives you a sense of accomplishment. Even small goals are important. Having goals helps to direct you toward the future.

Take action. Don't just wish your problems would go away or try to ignore them. Instead, figure out what needs to be done, make a plan to do it, and then take action.

Maintain perspective. Don't compare your situation to that of somebody you think may be worse off. You'll probably feel guilty for being down about your own problems. Rather, look at your situation in the larger context of your own life, and in relation to the world. Keep a long-term perspective and know that your situation can improve if you actively work at it.

Nurture a positive view of yourself. Developing confidence in your ability to solve problems and trusting your instincts helps build resilience.

HOW NOT TO FEEL SORRY
FOR YOURSELF

*Navigating the spectrum from sympathy
to compassion fatigue...*

Marsha was someone who believed that one of the main purposes and benefits of friendship was to have people with
whom she could share her troubles, people who would give her
sympathy.

Over time, she noticed that there were fewer welcome mats at
the doors of those friends and that her personal phone conversations and e-mail correspondence had diminished considerably. I
suggested that she explore this development by seeking out feedback about why people appeared to be keeping their distance.

Her inquiry revealed that her friends were indeed shying away,
because Marsha had become a "downer." Her constant expressions of gloom had led to social consequences. They told her that
she had gotten too "heavy" for them and that they wished that she
would work on her issues primarily in her therapy, rather than
when she was out socializing with them.

We all know people who seem mired in their misery and who
appear unable or unwilling to free themselves from their despair.
They are the friends, family members, or coworkers who seem

overly focused on their problems, grievances, and unhappiness. While their life complaints may be valid and legitimate, they are all about what is wrong. They seem to have "woe is me" playing as their life's theme song.

Some people are chronic self-pitiers who invariably find new reasons to feel sorry for themselves, rather than looking for ways to change their situations. It can be very difficult to be empathic toward these individuals since they inspire guilt or cause a reaction commonly referred to as "compassion fatigue." These people often are inconsolable and unresponsive to help or encouragement from others, even though they appear to want that from anyone who will listen to their troubles.

Marsha used the feedback well. In addition to "only having one therapist instead of several," she became more alert to her tendency to use friends in order to unload her despair and gain sympathy. She responded to my efforts to help her appreciate the many things in her life for which she might feel grateful and she joined a support group of people who shared some of the difficulties that were undermining her overall well-being.

In moderation and as a temporary device, self-sorrow can be soothing and helpful in one's efforts to overcome the pain that life sometimes causes. Sympathy and expressions of concern can be very healing and restorative for those who are suffering from a terrible life event or personal loss. However, when self-pity becomes extreme and constant, otherwise sympathetic people grow weary and resentful and may lose respect for the chronic sufferer who seems to be doing little or nothing to handle their troubles differently.

SAYING NO AND ACCEPTING NO

*Denying a request is not the same
as denying a relationship...*

Many people find it very difficult to say no or to accept someone else saying no to them without experiencing negative emotions. As a result, they often say yes when they really mean the opposite, which leads to consequences like anger and resentment directed toward themselves and others. A young patient of mine who said yes to six suitors who asked her to the high school senior prom is a memorable example.

Assertive people examine a request made of them or an offer made to them by assessing whether they believe it is reasonable or acceptable. They do not commit themselves to a yes or no reply until they fully understand what is being asked of them and whether or not they want to or are able to do it. If the answer to a request is no, they say so with firmness, clarity, and simplicity—often by just stating the word no by itself.

People who feel guilty when they wish to or have to say no often do so apologetically or with long-winded explanations or excuses that suggest they feel they are doing something unacceptable or wrong. This sometimes invites the person making the request to apply pressure in pursuit of the yes they are seeking until they succeed in getting it. When someone senses ambivalence, they will often request, or even demand, an explanation. Perhaps the best way to respond under these uncomfortable circumstances is by saying "because that's my answer" or "because that's what I think is best for me." Saying no should be seen as an honorable response and one that you are entitled to make even if it will not please someone else.

There are several strategies to help make it easier to say no when doing so is necessary or in your best interests. One way is to buy time, to provide yourself with an opportunity to decide whether you actually want to do something without the pressure of answering on the spot. Another strategy is to say no in an empathic way so that you lessen the likelihood of upsetting someone you care about who will be disappointed with your reply. "I wish that I could, but I can't help you this time" may be more comfortable for both parties than a simple no, and can ease a rejection that you may have wished to avoid.

Some people have strengthened their ability to refuse someone when necessary by practicing saying no when there is less at stake. Saying no to the telemarketer who calls at dinnertime is a favorite practice target.

Accepting no for an answer is also a difficult interpersonal experience for many of us. Each time you hear someone say no to a request that you have made, think to yourself, "I am not being rejected as an individual; it is my request that is being rejected." Rejection may come up emotionally because your need for approval is strong. You view acceptance of your request as an acceptance and approval of you; it is not.

WHY AM I SHY?

Techniques for handling social anxiety...

"Better to remain silent and be thought a fool than to speak up and remove all doubt" is a saying attributed to Abraham Lincoln. This negative belief is often held by people who grow nervous in social situations. They become convinced that they will say something foolish, thereby justifying their feelings of social ineptitude.

People who suffer from shyness or social anxiety are probably not enjoying life as much as possible. They feel nervous and unsure too much of the time and focus on avoiding much-feared rejection rather than looking for ways to have satisfying social experiences. Shyness is extremely common. In my research, I've seen that roughly 40 percent of the population complains about problems with shyness. It's a universal experience, and almost everyone has felt shy or socially anxious at some point in life.

Shyness is characterized by the desire to present a positive image in a social situation, combined with the fear that a negative or undesirable impression will be made. People who struggle with shyness have concerns about how they will be perceived by others. This leads them to withdraw from social situations in order to protect themselves. Rather than risk embarrassment and rejection, shy people would prefer to make no impression at all and avoid social situations where these dreaded moments might occur. Sadly, this avoidance interferes with their efforts to achieve the very things they desire most: good friends, intimacy, and feelings of social competence and social success.

Ironically, the fear that shy people have of not making a good impression may be well-founded. Avoidance of social interaction may prevent them from learning how to present themselves favorably, resulting in a self-defeating cycle. The fear of social awkwardness and humiliation leads to avoidance of social situations—the very opportunities people need to help them overcome their fears.

Whatever source of help one chooses, it is important to know there are ways to overcome problematic social anxiety. Some people handle their social anxiety by struggling through social interactions, doing the best they can, and always hoping that their fears will be less than they have been in prior situations. Others, for whom shyness or social anxiety feels more overwhelming or even debilitating, choose to work on their problem in psychotherapy. Some seek the benefits of anti-anxiety medication, while many choose a combination of therapy and medication to address their problem.

Exposure therapy is considered one of the most effective ways to help overcome severe social anxiety. This type of therapy became popular when first introduced as a way to help people who were phobic about air travel. The anxious individual is exposed to the source of fear and helped to reduce their anxiety under the guidance of a helping professional.

Another approach is social skills training, in which the anxiety sufferer meets with a professional therapist to discuss and rehearse problematic social situations. Making eye contact, handling small talk, and tolerating conversational silences are among the issues worked on to increase self-confidence and reduce anxiety.

SNATCHING DEFEAT FROM
THE JAWS OF VICTORY

Why we're often our own worst enemies...

After several tries, Jim, age twenty-five, was finally accepted into a prestigious bank management program. Once in the program, however, Jim found it difficult to make time to study. Assignments were handed in late, if even completed at all, and Jim developed severe headaches, all of which eventually led to his being the only trainee to leave the program...just days before he would have been forced to withdraw.

Alice, a first-year student in the PhD program in psychology at New York University, had a similar experience. An unusually hard-working and effective person, she found it easier to help others than to help herself. A cherished friend, colleague, and fellow student, Alice consistently failed to handle the demands of the graduate program despite a well-demonstrated ability for academic work. While ably helping fellow students with their work, she neglected or mishandled her own papers and presentations to the point where her status in the program became jeopardized.

Both Jim and Alice exhibit what might be described as self-defeating behaviors—clusters of thoughts, ideas, and actions that often sabotage success at work and in relationships. Self-defeating behaviors include a broad spectrum of self-imposed handicaps and other ploys and tactics that may suggest emotional trouble.

The obvious question that arises in situations like these is: Why exactly do these people become their own worst enemies?

Many explanations have been proposed for these behaviors. The most traditional analysis claims that people who repeatedly "shoot themselves in the foot" fear success, feel guilty about their behavior, or simply suffer from low self-esteem. Newer explanations include the possibility that self-defeatists have inflated opinions of themselves and that they use self-defeat as a way to take control of a fear of failure. Perhaps Jim had serious doubts about his ability to successfully make it through the bank management program, so his being "too busy" to find the time to study, as well as his headaches, provided excuses that justified his exit without having to risk failing in the actual program.

Alice might have been handling her anxieties about the graduate program by developing a praiseworthy excuse for her own self-doubts and conflicts about her performance. If her sacrifices on behalf of her fellow students led to her inability to successfully complete the program, she could take comfort in the belief that she would have succeeded if only she would have finished. Her self-defeating handicap protected her from the risk of failure.

Perhaps the best way that someone can stop self-defeating behaviors is to learn to reflect rather than react. When faced with the consequences of negative behavior, the question to ask oneself is, "If I could do this over again, what would I do differently?" The answer may be the most effective way to prevent self-defeat.

PRIDE OR BOASTFULNESS?

What's the difference?

There appears to be widespread confusion between what constitutes healthy pride, something one ought to be able to freely express when appropriate, and boastfulness or bragging, something most people find objectionable in themselves and others. Boastfulness is commonly defined as talking in a self-admiring way or glorifying oneself. It is often thought of as excessive pride. We tend to think of people who boast as arrogant, self-preoccupied, or perhaps insecure, which may be why they need to boast in the first place.

Pride, on the other hand, is generally defined as a feeling of self-respect and personal worth or a feeling of satisfaction with one's own (or another's) achievements. Most would agree that pride is a vital part of an individual's sense of self and an important component of healthy, positive self-esteem.

In my work as a psychotherapist, I often find myself helping patients make the distinctions discussed above. Many of us were taught as children, for better or worse, not to boast or brag, since this is regarded as an unattractive or off-putting behavior. "Don't be too big for your britches" and "Keep that up and you'll get a swelled head" are among the admonitions many of us remember from the past.

The problem is that our parents may not have understood the difference between boastfulness and expressions of healthy pride. This may explain why I so often hear qualifiers or apologetic preambles like: "I'm really doing very well at my new job! I don't want you to think I'm bragging, or anything." Or, "Please don't hear this the wrong way, but I'm really proud of my raise and promotion." Another patient recently told me that she won a prestigious award in her industry but had not shared the news with anyone but me because, as she put it, "I don't want anyone to think that I'm one of those braggarts with a head too big for my hat!"

It sometimes appears that the long-standing and well-cultivated internal restrictions against healthy, normal pride need to be dismantled and replaced. Everyone should be able to express pleasure in their personal or professional achievements without having to worry about being perceived as a show-off or braggart or being told to stop "crowing like a rooster and strutting around the farm!" "I'm really pleased with my raise and promotion, and I wanted to share it with you," seems a reasonable way to convey satisfaction and pride. It is not boastful, since it is not designed to claim the high ground or superiority to another. It is simply an expression of good feelings about one's accomplishment.

We should all have a way to voice our healthy satisfaction in our own accomplishments. Healthy pride can certainly be distinguished from boastfulness or bragging. We should never deny ourselves the right to "toot our own horn" when, in fact, that is exactly what we are entitled to do.

COMPLICATED MOURNING

Is there a wrong way to grieve?

There are many different kinds of grief. Uncomplicated or normal grief is characterized by a number of feelings, beliefs, and behaviors that most people experience after a significant loss. Those who suffer a loss of a loved one usually experience sadness, and often guilt and self-reproach. Anxiety, fatigue, helplessness, and shock are also common components of a normal grief reaction. The intensity and extent of these reactions may vary, but none is viewed as pathological.

People grieve in many different ways and with varying levels of intensity.

Differences in grief reactions are determined by a number of factors. Who the person was in relation to the griever is a major determinant of a grief response. The strength of the attachment is another influential factor, as is the mode of death. Grieving the sudden death of a young child, for example, will most likely be very different from grieving for an elderly relative who succumbed after a lengthy illness.

Problems occur when grief becomes excessive in intensity or persists for an abnormally long time. This is known as "complicated grief," and it can occur in a variety of ways. A chronic grief reaction is one that lasts for an exceptionally long time and never appears to come to a satisfactory resolution. The grieving individual responds to a loss from long ago with the full intensity and sadness one might anticipate from a much more recent loss.

Delayed grief is a response to a loss that gets postponed to a later time. The person suffering may be so overwhelmed by their feelings that they react in a way that seems insufficient at the time of the loss. This form of grief is often recognizable when we see someone have an extreme reaction to someone else's loss or to a movie or play in which a character in the story experiences a loss like theirs. It is as though their own grief catches up with them and they react in a manner that would have been expected at the time of the actual loss.

Another example of complicated grief is a masked grief reaction. Many people experience physical symptoms that are vague, have no identifiable cause, and are not recognized as related to the loss. For some reason, their grief at the time of the loss was absent or its expression was inhibited. As a result, their grieving process was never completed and caused complications that surface later in the form of physical symptoms or maladaptive behavior. Most often, symptoms like these abate after their feelings about the loss are dealt with in a more satisfactory way. Unexplained depression, for example, is often related to a loss experience from which someone has not adequately recovered.

For normal grief reactions, time and one's own resources are most often sufficient for us to recover from a loss. For complicated grief reactions, reaching out for help may be necessary to achieve a satisfactory resolution.

HANDLING MISTAKES AND FAILURES

The value in tolerating frustration and delaying gratification...

Different people have different ways of handling mistakes and failures. Some people who make a mistake or experience failure of one kind or another will see to it that they avoid the situation or circumstance in which it occurred. Others respond by ensuring that they learn something from the experience and try where possible not to repeat it.

Marcy, a new patient of mine, recently failed an exam (by two points) that she took in order to become licensed as a Certified Social Worker in New York State. While understandably disappointed, Marcy unfortunately responded by becoming severely self-critical. She questioned whether or not she had "the right stuff" to become a mental health professional—a career for which she had been preparing since college. Sadly, the lesson Marcy came away with was "I guess I'm just not smart enough to pass an exam like this. Maybe I'm not cut out to be a mental health professional."

The right lesson would have sounded more like this: "Okay, I blew this exam. I guess I'll have to work harder to prepare for the next one and figure out a way to do better. After all, I only need two more points. These things happen. I'll do better next time." One of the main reasons people fail to derive any benefit from their mistakes and failures is that they turn against themselves when such experiences occur, rather than learning something that will help them grow or change.

A major consequence for some people when they make a mistake or fail in some way is to focus only on self-critical feelings that can lead to sadness or depression. This may make it much more difficult to have the confidence to get back into the situation in which they experienced problems. Sometimes self-flagellation is a way to make a preemptive strike against oneself before anyone else does. The important point here is this: If you must, hate the fact that you made a mistake or endured a failure, but don't hate yourself for having done so.

We've all been through experiences where we found it difficult to tolerate the frustration of learning something new, where mistakes and failures were an unavoidable part of the process. This explains why so many adults never learn to ride a bicycle or swim and why so many youngsters spend six days, rather than six years, in Little League baseball.

Perhaps the most useful lesson to be learned from the experience of failure is to take something of value with you that can be helpful in dealing with similar situations in the future. Tolerating frustration and delaying gratification in the process of learning new things and striving for excellence are the hallmarks of a healthy, rational, and potentially successful child or adult.

THE PROBLEM WITH HAPPINESS

There's a correlation between
contentment and how well we cope
with life's demands...

ric Hoffer, the American social writer and philosopher, once
said, "The search for happiness is one of the chief sources of
unhappiness." Similarly, John Stuart Mill, the British philosopher
and economist, advised, "Ask yourself whether you are happy, and
you cease to be so." The pursuit of happiness, it seems, continues
to be a consuming enterprise for many people, especially those who
have found the state of happiness—as they define it—an elusive
goal. Our definition of happiness may be key to understanding the
primary reason why so many claim to either not be happy or not
really know if they are. Some believe that happiness is the natural
outcome of its commonly identified predecessors—namely, health
and wealth. However, experience tells us that the anticipated trio
of health, wealth, and happiness is often not realized.

It is a common scene in psychotherapy offices: bewildered and
confused people wondering why they are not happy when, in their
judgment, they have all of the necessary components for happiness. Many tend to believe that happiness is primarily a function of
positive external factors and circumstances, like health and wealth.

If this were generally true, then we would expect the wealthy to be happy and the poor to be the opposite. Obviously, we know this not to be the case. I have heard patients wonder why they don't seem to be as happy as their less well-off neighbor or less well-paid colleague at the office.

Scientists have come up with interesting findings from their research on this subject. One is that money does little to make us happier once our basic needs are met. Another is that marriage and faith lead to happiness (or that happy people are more likely to be married and spiritual). They have also concluded that temperamental "set points" for happiness—a predisposition to stay at a certain level of happiness—account for a large percentage of our feelings of well-being.

If one defines happiness as the absence of problems in life, as some do, then happiness—as so defined—is unlikely to be realized. If, on the other hand, happiness is at least partly defined as an excellent ability to handle life's problems when they occur, achieving a state of happiness has a chance.

My belief has long been that a major component of happiness is the extent to which a person can cope with the demands facing them, get through difficulties with minimal or no loss of self-esteem, and generally feel capable and competent as they proceed through life and its constant challenges. Those who struggle with worry and dread and see life as a harsh and unforgiving obstacle course are less likely to feel fulfilled and satisfied and, therefore, less likely to report being happy. For some, the greatest challenge of all may be to move from the beliefs, attitudes, and ideas that are associated with unhappiness to those that are more likely to lead to states of happiness as we best understand and define it.

BEING KIND TO YOURSELF

*Do you treat others better than you
treat yourself?*

Sara, a patient who has consulted me frequently for help for many years, has been a harsh self-critic, essentially picking up where her parents left off. While therapy has helped her to become more accepting of her shortcomings and occasional failures, Sara still, at times, can berate or belittle herself for an occasional error in judgment, a social gaffe, or even a disappointing experience on a blind date.

Louis, new to psychotherapy, was referred to me by his doctor, who picked up on the fact that Louis appeared to be particularly self-deprecating and did not miss an opportunity to describe a failure or negative experience of which he believed himself to be the likely cause. Physical symptoms as well as self-esteem issues were among the consequences of Louis's way of relating to himself.

Currently, there is considerable research being done in the area of what is called "self-compassion," i.e., how kindly people view themselves. It is commonly observed that many people are much more understanding, tolerant, and supportive of others than they ever are of themselves. When I hear clients being self-critical or demonstrating a lack of self-compassion, I will frequently ask how they imagine they might have responded to the identical situation if it involved their child or other close relative or friend instead of themselves. Not surprisingly, words of support and understanding flow freely from their lips, but not when they are the person in question.

Louis and Sara both provide good examples. Recently, Louis was a keynote speaker at a conference where he addressed an audience of over five hundred people. Despite the fact that he is an accomplished speaker and usually quite comfortable in front of large audiences, this time he became very anxious and, as a result, experienced difficulty giving his talk. A quiver in his voice, perspiration, and a number of misspoken words upset him deeply and unleashed a torrent of self-criticism, bordering on self-directed verbal abuse. When I asked him how he might have responded to his wife if this had happened to her, he immediately replied, "I'd probably tell her that it was not the end of the world...things like this happen...and she just has to take it in stride and try to do better next time."

Sara, having regained some of the pounds she lost during a successful weight-loss effort, berated herself for her lack of willpower, her poor self-discipline, and other perceived weaknesses and shortcomings that she believed led to her difficulties with weight control. What if this had been her daughter? You guessed it. The first words in her reply were, "It's okay, honey."

The research suggests that giving ourselves a break and accepting our imperfections and personal difficulties may be the first step toward better health. According to a February 28, 2011 *New York Times* article by Tara Parker-Pope on this subject, people who score high on tests of self-compassion have less depression and anxiety, and tend to be happier and more optimistic.

Some people, unfortunately, equate being hard on themselves with maintaining high standards of behavior and keeping themselves in line. This way of thinking suggests that if you "lighten up" on yourself by being more tolerant, understanding, and compassionate, you might become too easy on yourself and, therefore, be more prone to subpar performances and failures. There is no evidence to suggest that this is the case. There is evidence, however, that greater self-compassion is associated with better mental and physical health.

The field of self-compassion is still new and studies are underway to determine whether teaching self-compassion actually reduces stress, depression, and anxiety, and leads to more happiness and life satisfaction.

SELF-BLAME OR SELF-INQUIRY?

Fostering self-esteem despite the circumstances...

I n the course of one's life, many positive and negative things will occur that are unexpected and may be unexplained. We are, of course, delighted when the positive event comes our way that contributes something to our welfare, e.g., the unexpected raise or promotion at work, or a personal success such as a new romantic partnership. Negative events or developments, not surprisingly, are more difficult to process and for some require considerable effort to accept.

Diane was stunned when she was abruptly informed that she was being fired from her high-level executive position. She had enjoyed two successful years at her job and seemed well-liked by her senior colleagues and subordinates, so she could not understand why she was being let go without clear cause.

Ed, a divorced father of two young sons and a self-proclaimed "veteran of the dating wars," was thrilled to have met Kathy through a mutual friend and was thoroughly enjoying the positive progression of their new relationship. Unexpectedly, Kathy seemed to cool to Ed's further overtures and weeks later declared her wish to end their relationship. Ed's pursuit of an explanation for this sudden change seemed to fall on deaf ears as Kathy virtually disappeared from his life.

It is very understandable for people in situations like Diane's and Ed's to want to make sense of what occurred and to fill in the many blanks left open by the surprising actions of others. Arguably, occurrences like these are among the most difficult people face, for in addition to being shocking and bewildering, there may be nothing one can do about them. The only recourse may be to cope with the event in the best possible way.

Many people become self-critical or self-blaming in the course of their efforts to understand things that make no sense to them. People with self-esteem difficulties are especially vulnerable to self-blame and may develop explanations for negative events that inevitably make them feel even worse. This is best typified by conclusions like "It must be me," "I must have done something wrong," and "Maybe I was never adequate to begin with."

While self-blame is something to avoid, an inquiry by the injured person into what they might have done to contribute to their unfortunate circumstance might prove extremely helpful. Diane might ask whether anything she did led to her dismissal, so that she might learn something that could benefit her in the future. It is possible that through thoughtful inquiry she might discover her firing had little, if anything, to do with her. In Ed's case, similarly, rather than lick his wounds and disparage himself, he might discover something that would provide useful information for future romantic adventures. He might also come to realize that Kathy's abrupt ending of their relationship had a great deal to do with Kathy and little, if anything, to do with him.

Actual outcomes: Diane's boss felt that while her work was superior, her role in the organization needed to be filled by someone who was more aggressive. While no one else in the company agreed, he was the boss and did as he pleased. Diane was helped to discover this information through her inquiry, and she walked away with both her self-esteem and her dignity intact.

Once Ed moved past self-blame to a meaningful self-inquiry, he discovered the possibility that his own growing ambivalence about Kathy may have led him to behave differently in the relationship. This perhaps prompted her to find him less appealing than she had earlier, when he was very enthused and eager to be with her. It was helpful too to learn by chance that she had been having a hard time with her strong positive feelings and that had made it difficult for her to continue with him.

HANDLING RATHER THAN AVOIDING

Denial may provide temporary relief, but won't overcome the source of the fear...

I often hear patients express concern about an event or a situation of some kind for which they are experiencing something known as "anticipatory anxiety." This is a heightened sense of worry and vigilance about some dreaded event or experience that the anxious individual fears might be overwhelming. It is what I call the "what will happen next" fear.

There is a natural tendency to back away from things or situations that create tension. When someone suffers from anticipatory anxiety—whether it is a single episode or a form of chronic anxiety—avoidance may provide temporary relief, but not help overcome the source of the fear. Supportive friends and family often assist the sufferer in his or her efforts to avoid the source of distress whenever possible. Sometimes avoidance is seen as a reasonable response. If you can reduce or eliminate anxiety reactions by avoiding the feared object or situation, why not do so? This works adequately when the object of anxiety is easily avoidable for most people, e.g., snakes, spiders, or public speaking. In other cases, avoidance is unrealistic, as in fears of heights, elevators, flying, or dogs.

One of the treatment options for avoidance anxiety is exposure therapy. This involves exposure to the feared stimulus in a safe and controlled setting, frequently the therapist's office. The patient is subjected to the feared stimulus as part of the therapeutic process. One simple form of exposure therapy is systematic desensitization, where exposure is gradually increased until the person is immersed in the feared situation. Gradually the anxiety recedes and the fear itself fades away. This method of treatment is not for everyone, but for some, it can be very effective. It is the classic form of overcoming a fear by handling it rather than avoiding it. Another therapeutic intervention that promotes managing a fear is modeling. In modeling, the patient observes others (the "models") who are responding in a relaxed way to the presence of the feared stimulus. The patient is encouraged to imitate the models, thereby reducing the patient's own avoidant response to the fear.

Claire entered therapy for a variety of problems, but her fear of riding in elevators was her greatest concern and the first issue she wished to tackle in therapy. Her fear had been present for several years and she believed it to be traceable to a friend's experience of being stuck in an elevator for over an hour in a New York City building. The friend shared her frightening experience in graphic detail and Claire said, "I haven't been the same since." Claire's handling of this fear consisted primarily of avoidance. For her, this meant walking up and down twenty-two flights of stairs to her office in a Manhattan skyscraper, living in a three-story brownstone building, and staying in hotels with escalator access to low-floor rooms. Exposure treatment, which involved Claire spending many sessions with me near an elevator and eventually in it, was initially overwhelming for her, but in the end it worked. She successfully tolerated her anxiety, which gradually diminished with repeated exposure. After years of avoidance, Claire felt the predictable empowerment of having truly overcome a fear by achieving mastery, rather than just "getting by" through the stressful and extraordinarily limiting avoidance of elevators.

There are countless conflict situations that require a direct approach and the courage to confront, rather than avoid. Where appropriate, patients find ways to handle the difficulties that they are confronting in their lives, rather than seek relief by avoiding them.

One of the important objectives of therapy for many people is to learn effective ways of handling the difficult and complex challenges of life. Whether asking for a raise from a stern boss, discussing a grievance with a romantic partner, or any other situation that creates anxiety, directly handling matters will always be a more effective response than avoidance.

COMPLAINING

A communication made in the
hope that someone will recognize
our suffering....

Why do some people complain a great deal while others complain rarely, if ever? Is complaining learned behavior? Do complainers come from a long line of complainers? Is the need to complain determined by the troubles one experiences in life or is it more or less unrelated to how good or bad things are for the particular individual? Does complaining have a purpose that we need to understand better? What are the differences between complaining and simply sharing one's troubles with someone? The answers to these and similar questions might help us understand and, therefore, better tolerate this means of communicating that many of us find unpleasant or even objectionable.

For some people, complaining about things provides some measure of relief from the many life stresses they experience. Complaining can get attention, reassurance, and sympathy; it can feel validating, especially when the listener agrees with what troubles the complainer.

Other people who are heard to complain a great deal may do so because they have many troubles. However, there are those who complain a lot yet, from our observations, it doesn't really seem as though much is wrong. Then there are those who never complain but whose lives seem extremely troubled. Perhaps complaining is actually only loosely related to justifiable difficulties; perhaps it doesn't have much to do with them at all. My observations are that the need to complain is determined by factors other than what is or is not occurring in the life of the complainer.

Two patients of mine provide good illustrations of this concept. Martha, a sixty-eight-year-old, suffered from cancer for several years before her death. Her final years were characterized by considerable pain and periodic hospitalizations, and her life was consumed with the oversight and management of this horrible disease. Despite this, I never once heard Martha complain. Instead, she expressed gratitude for the many healthy years she enjoyed prior to her illness, celebrated the successes and joys of family and friends, and expressed compassion for the many she believed suffered a fate much worse than her own. Her way of handling herself under such difficult circumstances—right up to the end of her life—was widely admired by everyone who knew her.

Tamara was a different story altogether. Her complaining was panoramic and continuous and perhaps a reason why she had fewer friends than she would have liked—ironically, one of her major complaints. For her, complaining seemed a way of life and not just a means of communicating with the outside world. Minor frustrations and disappointments were complained about and one was led to wonder how Tamara would cope if something like serious illness or job loss were to occur in her life, like it has for so many others.

It appears that complaining, for many, is a communication made in the hope that someone will recognize their suffering. Once recognition is achieved, something inside the complainer feels satisfied. For some, this ends their complaining. For others, their complaining is ongoing and unresponsive to any intervention on the part of others. I suppose these are the people for whom complaining is a way of life, as it represents an attempt at achieving satisfaction even though it is often unsuccessful.

There certainly are differences between complaining and sharing or discussing matters with others. Discussing a situation tends to involve an attempt to understand the origin of a problem and think of a remedy. We assume responsibility for what bothers us, rather than blaming others or outside factors. The discussion may provide new perspective on a situation, thereby helping us to deal with it more effectively.

Perhaps the words attributed to the 8th-century Buddhist scholar and monk Shantideva would serve as good counsel: "If something can be changed, work to change it. If it cannot, why worry, be upset, and complain?"

SORE LOSERS

Winning and self-esteem...

There are people for whom losing anything at all is a major negative event with all kinds of troubling consequences. Others seem to be able to take a loss in stride and file it away as a minor disappointment that has little overall impact on their lives. Researchers have found that older children and adults who are sore losers worry about what others think of them if they don't win, or feel that winning is what makes them good people. (Interestingly, this confusion of doing something good with being someone who is good is typical of how toddlers think.)

It seems to me that the problem here is the extent to which people see winning and losing as some sort of test of their self-worth. If, as appears to be the case, a person involved in a competition of some sort requires a victory in order to feel adequate or competent, the likelihood that they can tolerate a loss is significantly lessened.

Often, these people do not have a way of assessing and evaluating wins and losses in accordance with their appropriate value and importance. Thus, the loss of a card game with a friend might be responded to no differently than the loss of an important promotion at work or the loss of an important athletic competition by a slim margin.

There are people who can play a board or card game and simply enjoy the experience without great emphasis on the outcome, i.e., whether or not they win or lose. When they lose at tennis, for example, they appreciate the opportunity to have played a favorite sport, value and emphasize the exercise benefits, and see the experience as an opportunity to improve their game, hoping that the next time might involve a victory. Others—the proverbial sore losers—respond quite differently. They tend to look for excuses to explain their loss, blame others and outside circumstances for the defeat, and feel disappointed throughout the experience. They feel incapable of absorbing the loss without suffering.

Some of the possible reasons for the psychological evolution of the sore loser are likely established early in life by well-intentioned and well-meaning parents who might not have fully understood some of the ways to counter and avoid sore losing. Some parents place too much emphasis on winning, rather than on effort. Parents would do well to help their children be aware of their own experiences with losing or defeat, so that their children don't believe that they have to be perfect or victorious in order to be acceptable or adequate. Parents often let their children win at games at home in order to avoid upset or frustration. This may give the child a distorted idea about their ability, skill, or "luck." When these children play the game with friends and happen to lose, they may not be adequately prepared for the experience and may react problematically.

Another way parents can help their children is to encourage them not to give up when they lose at something. There are children, for example, who no longer wish to play a game if they are initially unsuccessful at it. Some parents, unfortunately, accept this too readily and find a sport where their child can excel with more ease or, worse, allow them to give up sports altogether. Emphasizing effort and rewarding perseverance are what is called for here.

No one really likes a sore loser...most importantly, the sore losers themselves.

WORRYING

Anticipation as a form of preparedness...

Many familiar themes are raised in the course of a psychotherapy treatment hour. Family, career, relationship, health, and financial matters are a few examples among many, many others. Patients often seek assistance in understanding and addressing their specific concerns, and resolving the conflicts and other difficulties that develop in the course of their demanding and complex lives.

Among the many things that have aroused my curiosity is the question of why some people worry about these issues, while others seem to attend to them in various ways, but do not worry about them. Certainly, and perhaps obviously, people who are more prone to feeling anxious are more likely to be worriers than people who rarely experience anxiety symptoms. This, however, does not take the matter far enough to satisfy me. I am interested in why even some patients who are generally not anxious by nature seem to worry at times, and about certain issues, but not others.

My informal research during treatment sessions represented an attempt to learn more about worrying behavior, while always trying to help my patients understand, manage, and, where possible and appropriate, eliminate worry from their emotional repertoire.

I wondered to what extent worrying is a voluntary or an involuntary behavior. I wondered, too, regardless of whether worrying was or was not a choice, whether it had some purpose that I did not fully understand. Was it ever constructive and helpful or, as I have long believed, did it simply create emotional stress and serve no healthy purpose?

To clarify, my comments and observations about worrying are not about things that would realistically arouse a worry response in anyone. Awaiting the results of a biopsy of a suspicious growth or learning that your home might be in the path of a predicted tornado are worrisome events for anyone. However, some people worry about becoming destitute when there appears to be no rational basis for this particular threat to their welfare. Others worry about their health, even though they have no symptoms of any kind and demonstrate no particular vulnerability to life-threatening illness. The list is endless. Some people seem to worry about everything and others about nothing really at all.

One interesting discovery that emerged from my informal research was that some people, it seems, worry as a form of preparedness. The belief is that one will be ready or better prepared for a dreaded event if one worries about it. This, it is often believed by the worrier, will prevent being caught off guard, stunned, or somehow negatively affected in some way by that event. In other words, if one worries that they will hear terrible news from their physician following a routine medical appointment, then they will be less upset when the news is delivered than if they had not worried at all. If a student worries about an important exam, the expectation is that finding out they did poorly or failed will somehow be less troubling because they were "prepared" for this possibility by virtue of many days or weeks of anticipatory worrying.

It seems to me that worrying as a means of preparation or "upset avoidance" is an unhappy illusion. It stimulates pessimism and dread. It validates negative beliefs about whatever one is worried about and makes it appear as though worry is appropriate, even necessary.

Probably the best approach to events like those described above is to do what is possible to reduce the erroneous belief that one needs to "get ready" for worst-case scenarios. This is especially important since these scenarios may exist only in one's mind, and are not necessarily part of an actual experience...or ever need to be. Rational and realistic self-talk appears to work well for many people as a way to challenge automatic worrying when it occurs.

Worry may be harder to control or diminish once it "kicks in" than when one can "nip it in the bud" by successfully convincing oneself that it is unnecessary. This is the difference between repair and prevention—the latter, of course, always being preferable to the former.

FEARS, FEELINGS, AND FACTS

*How can we retain our perspective
under stress?*

There is a strong tendency on the part of many people to confuse fears, feelings, and facts. In therapy sessions, I often hear statements like these: "I am definitely not going to get that promotion (raise, award, scholarship, etc.)." "She is not going to want to go out with me again!" "There is no way I will get that mortgage I applied for." Certainly, there may be validity to some of these assertions or beliefs, but I wonder why optimism or hopefulness is missing when these individuals express themselves. Why are they not saying things like "I hope I get that promotion," or "I would like to think she'll go out with me again"?

People who suffer from depression tend to see much of life through a "dark" lens and are prone to doomful-sounding predictions and beliefs. Another reason why people worry and may be pessimistic is because they believe that worrying or imagining negative outcomes will prepare them if and when their negative predictions come true. In "Worrying," I suggested that when people are negative in order to prepare for a presumed negative occurrence, all that really happens is that they make themselves miserable. They are no more prepared for hurt or disappointment than if they had found a way to be hopeful instead. In fact, they probably would have been better off being hopeful, since we know that optimism—as opposed to its opposite outlook—is associated with general well-being and better overall mental health.

A major problem with treating fearful predictions or worries as though they were facts is that the person might be prone to behaving as though the feared disappointment or rejection has already occurred and acting accordingly.

A former patient's experience illustrates this phenomenon. Linda, an unemployed elementary school teacher, was asked to try out for a new position by subbing for the regular teacher who was on a two-week sick leave. While believing she performed reasonably well, Linda expressed certainty that she did not get the job: "I *know* I did not impress them and I *know* that I will not get the job... I just KNOW!" Unfortunately, Linda found ways to feed her pessimism. She was told she would hear within a week or ten days. By day three, she was further convinced: "If they really wanted me, they would have called immediately and not waited." She was treating her fear like a fact and, therefore, handled matters as though she had already been rejected for the position. I discovered in a subsequent session that she had been slow to submit additional information requested by the school and managed to "forget" to write the thank-you note she had promised. She acted as though it no longer mattered what she did or did not do since, as far as she was concerned, she had already been rejected for the position. I was pleased when she won the position fourteen days after her tryout—not only because she needed the job in order to support her family, but also because it was a powerful life lesson and she learned a great deal about herself and her self-defeating proclivities.

Obviously, whether you are an optimist by nature or a pessimist instead, it is important to keep perspective—especially under stressful circumstances—and differentiate your fears and beliefs from presumed reality, so that you do not act in ways that are self-defeating or, worse, self-destructive.

➤ See also WORRYING, page 44
YET, page 69

I CAN'T AFFORD *THAT*

*Are we substituting financial concern
for something unrelated that we need
to address?*

In my psychotherapy practice, I have worked with people who run the gamut from those who are exceptionally wealthy to those who can barely survive on their very limited resources.

The subject of money and its role in people's lives comes up frequently in sessions and in a variety of ways, aside from the issue of the fee for the therapy itself. With individuals, the concerns tend to center around the cost of living reasonably well in New York City and managing the familiar demon of financial debt.

With couples, the worries are much the same; however, a common debate occurs when different priorities and values create conflict between marital partners regarding what is and is not affordable.

Money issues, too, are often an indirect means of expressing other beliefs and fears that people hold, perhaps without being consciously aware of them. One example of this phenomenon was apparent in the therapy of a wealthy investment banker who, despite his high six-figure annual income, told me that he was convinced it was impossible to afford to raise a child in New York City.

The many people he knew who were raising one or more children in the city on a fraction of his income had no impact on him whatsoever. Further therapeutic investigation of this rather curious and strongly held belief revealed a man who was frightened of becoming a father. This attitude was traceable to his own painful history as a child in an unstable and unhappy family. "I can't afford to raise a child" really had nothing to do with money. He could afford a child financially, but not emotionally. He was helped by being able to recognize how a long-held "money issue" had nothing really to do with money at all.

Another patient informed me that despite his need to take up an exercise program for health reasons, he was not able to afford a membership at a local gym because the $900 annual membership fee (which could be paid at $75 per month) was "way too expensive" for him. It was helpful that I happened to know that this same patient thought nothing of frequently ordering $150 bottles of wine when he ate out several times each month! He had never made the "can afford/can't afford" connection.

Another patient complained in a marital therapy session that a raise for the nanny (whom he did not particularly care for) was "out of the question" since it was "a budget-buster." When reminded by his wife of the price he paid for two tickets to the World Series for himself and his son ($900 each!), he realized how little the issue being discussed was money-related.

There are many more examples like this. I treated a man who "couldn't afford" a vacation involving air travel, who was actually deeply afraid of flying. There was the woman who claimed "financial hardship" made it "impossible" to pay an entry fee to a social event who was terrified of the rejection she might suffer if she attended. There was a patient who could "no longer afford" the training program in which he was struggling to survive when he was actually wrestling with a fear of failure.

We are all vulnerable to making judgments such as the ones described above. It is especially helpful and self-enlightening when we dig a little deeper in order to determine whether we are being truly honest with ourselves or substituting money concerns for a different and entirely unrelated issue—perhaps one that we need to address with a mind toward personal growth and change.

WHAT IF AND SO WHAT?

Worry and dread may not prepare us
for the worst-case scenarios...

Recently, a patient in my psychotherapy practice was reflecting on her experience in therapy after what she described as three productive years of treatment. Laura was originally referred by her family physician when no medical cause could be identified to explain her various physical complaints and disrupted sleep, among other difficulties. She struggled with depression, was frequently anxious, and described herself as a chronic worrier who saw the world, essentially, through a bleak lens. She reported general unease with matters of daily living and appeared to have a hard time finding joy and satisfaction in her personal life or in her professional role as a museum curator.

Fortunately, Laura's psychotherapy accomplished many things, as she happily recounted in our final session together. She felt "stronger, more like the trunk of the tree than the fragile twig I was three years ago." She felt as though she had earned her "adult card" to go along with the other credit cards in her wallet. She believed that she had developed a more solid ability to cope with life's demands and expectations with less anxiety, and she generally felt more capable and competent, which for Laura included feeling better able to engage in a romantic partnership that survived beyond the initial dating phase.

Laura identified two particular accomplishments; something she relinquished during the course of her treatment and something she acquired as a tool that helped improve her coping skills. Laura believed that these were the two most important achievements of her course of psychotherapy.

In the beginning of her treatment, Laura would describe events in her life that she felt were "overwhelming," "stressful," "upsetting," or worse. Initially, she would be startled when often she would hear me react to a tale of woe by saying "So what?" or words to that effect. While not being insensitive or without compassion for Laura's unfortunate suffering, I was able to help her achieve perspective and appropriately diminish the negative impact of many everyday occurrences that had been so terribly unsettling for her. Laura claimed that her newly acquired ability to say "So what?" helped ease her anxiety and enabled her to take more things in stride than she had been able to three years earlier. The difficult and annoying supervisor, the very noisy neighbors who once enraged her, and the not-very-neat friend with whom she shared an apartment became less daunting or upsetting when "I could give them the 'so what' treatment," Laura happily told me.

The other therapeutic accomplishment Laura identified was her ability, over the course of our time together, to give up her "what ifs." Early on, she was filled with what we termed "anticipatory dread." This both created and perpetuated her highly stressful existence. It took the form of identifying worst-case scenarios, e.g., "What if he says no?" or "What if I fail the exam?" or "What if I have cancer?" She did this as a way of preparing for what she had convinced herself were the likely outcomes of almost anything that occurred in her life. When Laura understood that her worry and dread were not serving to prepare her for those worst-case scenarios as she had originally believed, she was able to gradually relinquish this troubled view of the future and found herself much less anxious and unhappy. To quote Laura, "No more 'What if?' and plenty of 'So what?' really set me free!"

➤ See also WORRYING, page 44

FEARS, FEELINGS, AND FACTS, page 47

ROAD AND SIDELINE RAGE

*What can you do as a person or
parent if you're subject to misplaced
anger and aggression?*

We've all seen them (or maybe some of us have been them). The driver on the highway who cuts us off or denies us entry into the lane. The driver who makes various hand gestures at us, believing—rightly or wrongly—that we have cut them off. What happens to so many of us that leads us to rant and rage on the road, behaving in ways that we normally condemn as unacceptable and inappropriate in adults? Is this any different from the behavior of the parent who becomes angry and aggressive at their child's soccer game?

According to a study by kinesiology PhD student Jay Goldstein of the University of Maryland School of Public Health, ego defensiveness, one of the triggers that ignites road rage, also kicks off parental "sideline rage," and a parent with a control-oriented personality is more likely to react to that trigger by becoming angry and aggressive.

By surveying parents at youth soccer games in suburban Washington, DC, Goldstein found that parents became angry when their egos got in the way. "When they perceived something that happened during the game to be personally directed at them or their child, they got angry," says Goldstein. "That's consistent with findings on road rage." Perhaps a telling example of this is how we experience the driver who cuts us off on the highway. We don't say, "He cut my car off." Instead, we say, "He cut *me* off." We take it as a personal affront, even an attack. Worse, we might experience the event as one in which we were bested, defeated, or made to feel weak and inadequate for allowing it to happen in the first place. Often, that response triggers a need for revenge or retaliation. Similarly, when a child performs poorly on the playing field, some parents see that moment as a reflection on them and become angry at the embarrassment or humiliation caused by that child. This is true, too, when a bad call by a game official feels like a personal attack on the child or the parent.

Goldstein discovered that the parents he defined as control-oriented were the ones more likely to take something personally and flare up at referees, opposing players, and their own kids than autonomy-oriented parents, who took greater responsibility for their own behavior. Fifty-three percent of the 340 parents he surveyed reported getting angry to some degree during their kids' soccer games. The targets of the anger were most often the referee and their own children's teams. Most parents reported experiencing only slight anger lasting for less than two minutes. About 40 percent of parents reported responding to their anger with actions that ranged from muttering to themselves to yelling and walking toward the field. Regardless of their personality type, all parents were susceptible to becoming more aggressive because of viewing actions on the field as affronts to them or their kids. The autonomy-oriented parents took longer to get angry as compared to the control-oriented parents.

What can you do if you see yourself as guilty of the types of anger and aggression described in this essay?

First, try to get *perspective* as quickly as you can and appreciate the moment for what it truly is: just someone driving aggressively or even irresponsibly who does not require a similar response from you, or a disappointing or negative moment in the game that does not concern you directly and, therefore, does not necessitate a public response, especially if you are upset or angry.

Second, if you are a parent, use the *presence* of your child, where possible. Remember that you are the parent and a responsible role model for your children, always and forever. Would you want your child exploding at the referee or raging at other drivers now or later in life?

Third, try to *replace* angry thoughts with rational ones. For example, remind yourself: "This is my child's game, not mine," and "This, too, shall pass."

PERSONAL DECISION-MAKING

*How can we know if we have
enough information to make the
best possible choice?*

In a recent treatment session, Kelli wanted my help in deciding whether or not she ought to continue dating Greg, the new man she met through an online dating website. At first, this seemed like a perfectly reasonable and appropriate issue to raise in therapy and invite my input. I listened intently as Kelli reported the conversations she had already had with many family members, friends, and colleagues about what she should do about her "problem." Not surprisingly, Kelli had become quite confused and more doubtful when she discovered that her respondents were about evenly divided regarding whether and how she should proceed with Greg.

When I asked Kelli what she thought she wanted to do about Greg, she looked startled and exclaimed, "I have no idea!" Kelli was unsure about her feelings regarding her new beau and, I discovered, had asked everybody what she should do—except herself! Kelli and I agreed that the real problem was less "what to do about Greg," than understanding why she seemed unable (or even unwilling) to figure this out for herself.

Kelli, like so many individuals struggling to make important life decisions, did not have much faith in her ability to make sound, reliable choices and decisions, especially of a personal nature. Raised by parents who valued obedience, compliance, and passivity, rather than independence, autonomy, and assertiveness, Kelli was criticized, often mercilessly, and developed into a person who magnified her own limitations and believed herself to be inferior to others. Procrastination, indecisiveness, and self-doubt are common consequences of an emotional climate like the one Kelli grew up in.

It was always difficult for Kelli to know her abilities and strengths, including whether or not she had the capacity to make reasoned judgments, sound choices, and reliable decisions. Her low self-esteem and chronic self-doubt were responsible for her overreliance on the presumed wisdom of others in knowing what was best for her. This explained her need to survey others for guidance in how to proceed in a new romantic relationship, as well as for so many other decisions affecting her young adult life.

What eventually changed for Kelli in the course of our work together was her appreciation for the fact that decisions like whether or not to deepen a romantic relationship, make a job or career change, move to a new apartment, and so many others were hers and hers alone. While appropriate input from trusted and informed others was helpful, the ultimate choice was hers and she needed to be able to make it, regardless of the outcome. It was also helpful for Kelli to no longer assess and evaluate her decisions based on the outcome of her choices. The decision to ask a boss for a raise, for example, ought not to be evaluated solely on whether or not the raise was given. Similarly, her decision to continue to see Greg could not only be related to how things eventually turned out between them.

Actual outcome: Kelli decided to continue seeing Greg. Four months later, she discovered that Greg had lied to her on a number of occasions and she decided to terminate the relationship—without asking anyone else what she should do. Fortunately, and to Kelli's credit, she did not blame herself for a bad decision in continuing to see Greg four months earlier, recognizing that she made a choice based on the available information she had at the time and based on her own criteria and judgment.

➤ See also SELF-BLAME OR SELF-INQUIRY?, page 32

FEARS, FEELINGS, AND FACTS, page 47

GOOD ENOUGH—
EXCELLENT—
PERFECT

When the struggle for perfection
obstructs our achievable goal...

The idea for this essay came from years of observing how people tend to utilize and relate to the three concepts in the title. Good enough, excellent, and perfect can be seen as degrees on a continuum, or as independent concepts or levels. The emotional significance placed on these terms can promote or interfere with personal satisfaction and success.

Frequently, patients will describe a person, an experience, or even themselves, using "perfect" as an ideal reference. Bob: "I don't want to get married until I find the perfect woman for me." Sheila: "My presentation to the board of directors has to be perfect." Arthur: "The play was okay, but it wasn't perfect." Jill: "My fiancé's parents are coming for dinner. I want the evening to be perfect."

Perfection references can be harmless and perhaps nothing more than an expression of enthusiasm or excitement. "I had the most perfect day yesterday at the museum!" "Everything at the surprise party went perfectly!" Problems may arise when the need for "perfect" creates disappointment or disillusionment and interferes with someone's ability to appreciate and enjoy excellent—or even good enough—achievement.

In therapy or counseling sessions, patients will sometimes hear me express concern when I hear "perfect" used in a way that I believe to be problematic. This often leads to an exploration of the patient's expectations and whether they are reasonable and realistic. "Perfect" dates usually aren't, of course, but some people experience this as profoundly disappointing or, worse, inadequate and unacceptable. Bob may never find someone to marry unless he can learn to accept the flaws, limitations, and foibles of others, as well as his own. Sheila may be putting excessive pressure on herself, thereby making it more difficult to develop an excellent presentation for her board of directors. I asked Arthur, an actor himself, to define a "perfect" play for me and he was able to appreciate the unrealistic nature of his expectations when he tried to do so. Fortunately, Jill was able to relax her self-demand for perfection and instead allowed a more spontaneous and enjoyable evening with her future in-laws.

Sometimes people really don't mean "perfect" when they use the term in discussing their lives, but many *do*—and they become deeply disappointed when their expectations are not met. Often, major decisions—some life-altering—are made because something does not pass the "perfect" test. Individuals who struggle to achieve perfection, as they define it, may be unable to work toward a more realistic and achievable goal: excellence. "I did the best I could" or "I gave an excellent speech" can and should replace "I was not good enough" or "My speech was not perfect." On some occasions, "good enough" may be an acceptable level of accomplishment or achievement, as well. Many believe that "good enough" is synonymous with inadequate and find it too far from perfect to be acceptable. Perhaps attempting to apply these three levels of evaluation to your own personal and professional lives will make them even more meaningful and enjoyable, especially if you are able to be realistic and fair to yourself and others in doing so.

PREMATURE QUITTING

How can we distinguish between self-care and giving up?

Bruce was as excited about his new relationship with Katie, a woman he met through an online dating service, as he was about his new job as a production assistant for a popular television talk show. His wild enthusiasm about both new endeavors was typical of Bruce, as was the predictable outcome for both experiences. Bruce was just fine as long as he continued to see Katie as the "perfect girlfriend," whom he described as "flawless." The same was true of "the best job in the world"—until both Katie and the job managed to cause some frustration or disappointment, at which point Bruce wanted to quit both of them. He was encouraged to explore his tendency to act this way, rather than simply repeat this behavior and, to his credit, was able to do so.

For some people, quitting comes too easily, too often, and applies to too many experiences in their lives. When excitement and novelty wear off, as invariably occurs with most things, those who have difficulty tolerating frustration or handling occasional or temporary boredom are ready to move on. Boredom and frustration are not the only reasons we quit too soon. When something we are engaged in proves too difficult and seems as though it could lead to humiliation and failure, we may convince ourselves that we are really not that interested anyway and quit. A person I know who finally fulfilled a long-standing desire to learn to play tennis found it difficult to tolerate the frustration of not achieving instant excellence after six lessons. He made the case for quitting by denigrating the sport, suddenly worrying about the potential for physical injury, and being "too busy" to continue his "inconvenient" lessons. Unfortunately, he could not or would not tolerate the road to mastery as a tennis player the way he had been able to tolerate the journey to a successful career as a patent attorney.

There are times, of course, when stopping something, as distinguished from quitting it, may be wise and well advised. It is important to recognize the differences between the two. Stopping implies a reevaluation of your decision to do or not do something for sound and valid reasons. Quitting implies giving up and releasing yourself from the burden of responsibility for your actions.

If any of the above-described behaviors applies to you, there are things you might do to help yourself.

First, recall the last time you quit something and review both the positive and negative consequences of having done so.

Second, look at your present situation and try to determine the wisdom or folly of quitting at this time.

Third, ask a trusted friend or colleague to review your choices in order to obtain a more objective view of your situation.

Finally, if you are inclined to quit something, ask yourself why and why now. Are the reasons justifiable or are you simply looking to avoid something unpleasant, such as embarrassment or boredom?

PERSONAL PROPAGANDA

The lies we tell ourselves...

" I meant to call you, but I didn't have time!" "I absolutely cannot afford the time for physical therapy!" "I'm not sure if I have the money to afford a babysitter." "There is nothing I could have done about it!" "No way can I find the time for lunch."

We all hear ourselves say these and many similar statements from time to time. Beliefs like the ones above are uttered with great certainty and are often the very ways in which we defeat ourselves and deny a more satisfying and fulfilling way of life. I refer to these oft-heard declarations as "personal propaganda." When I am able to be sufficiently self-aware and insightful in my own life, I try to challenge myself when I hear myself say, for example, "I don't have the time to work on that article," or "I'm much too busy to attend that conference."

As someone in the position of helping others, I frequently hear examples of such firmly held beliefs and find myself attempting to determine whether I am listening to self-defeating propaganda or whether there is a legitimate basis for the belief. The answer is often immediately obvious. The person who claimed not to be able to afford a babysitter on a Saturday night recently purchased a luxury convertible for his newly licensed teenage daughter. It is easy to observe, in this case, how one's values and preferences often guide judgment and beliefs about what is and is not affordable. Similarly, the patient who tried to convince me that there was "no way" he could afford to travel to a relative's wedding on the West Coast recently made a significant addition to his art collection. The examples are endless.

Two other common areas of trouble for those who say they don't have enough time are adequate sleep and healthy eating. So many of the symptoms or problems reported by sleep-deprived people would be eliminated—or at least eased—by getting more rest. Too often, however, the claim is that there is not enough time for that. This particular assertion is often traceable to the belief that sleep is a "waste of time" during which nothing productive or meaningful takes place. Similarly, busy people are often heard to justify poor eating or not eating at all because of the extraordinary demands of the job that leaves them no time for proper meals.

Perhaps by becoming more self-aware of our own "personal propaganda," we might have a better opportunity to successfully challenge some of our self-defeating behaviors.

➤ See also I CAN'T AFFORD *THAT*, page 50

YET

A negative future isn't the only possible outcome . . .

You might be surprised to learn that I think "yet" is one of the most important and powerful words in the English language. Its presence or absence from many conversations with patients in my practice is extremely revealing. I use the word "yet" in many sessions when I hear indications of pessimism, which, for some, comes much too easily about too many things.

I have been accused of being too optimistic when I tell patients that I am hopeful on their behalf, especially when, for various reasons, they express a negative or pessimistic outlook about some aspects of their lives where hopefulness would better sustain them.

Without a crystal ball, we cannot realistically predict the future, however much we try. There are, however, self-proclaimed experts on the future who claim to know exactly how things are likely to turn out. I have heard people make comments like the following: "I know that I will never find someone to marry!" "I am sure that I will never get the supervisory position…I just *know*!" "My spouse and I will never be able to work things out!" I am always struck by such declarations of doom from people who otherwise would agree—in more objective and rational moments—that they were being overly pessimistic and, worse yet, undermining the possibility that they could be wrong and that other potential outcomes also exist.

When I hear these declarations of doom from patients, especially early in the therapeutic adventure, I suggest to them that perhaps they might "borrow" my optimism until they—hopefully—are able to develop their own! I acknowledge that my optimism may not be entirely justified, since I am not always aware of all the reasons for their pessimism. Nonetheless, I am often heard to say things like: "I don't know enough yet to be able to completely sign on for your pessimism, so let me wait awhile before I join your despair!" or "I just met you and I've heard how terrible your situation is. However, you came here in the hope of some kind of change, so let's see what we might be able to do together before you return to the despair that preceded our efforts together."

Adding the word "yet" to pessimistic or doomful predictions often gets a patient's attention and introduces the possibility that their strong beliefs in a negative future outcome may not be entirely accurate. At least there is someone else—someone with some credibility—who is not ready to automatically accept his or her hopelessness.

"I know that I will never find someone to marry!" becomes "I haven't found someone to marry yet." "We will never be able to work things out!" becomes "We have not been able to work things out yet." No, there is nothing magical about adding this word, but it does introduce a measure of hope into the proceedings, without which a change effort may not fare well. Simply stated, people work toward change differently when they believe that change can actually occur.

When people view their situation as a condition, rather than a problem, they treat it differently and might not approach a change effort in the same way. Conditions are usually lived with, managed, coped with, etc. A problem is something to solve—or, at least, it should be. Being unhappily single or having a troubled marriage are best viewed as problems for which solutions might be actively sought, not conditions that are necessarily to be endured for a lifetime.

Yet. Perhaps you might find this word a useful addition to your own emotional vocabulary, especially when you observe pessimism interfering with your ability to be reasonably hopeful and optimistic when an outcome has yet to occur. It might even influence your attitude about an important issue in your life and lead to actions on behalf of meaningful change.

➤ See also PROBLEM OR CONDITION?, page 171
WORRYING, page 44
FEARS, FEELINGS, AND FACTS, page 47

Living

Our Relationship with Others

HANDLING CRITICISM

No matter how badly criticism hurts,
some good may come out of it . . .

f criticism were an object, some people would think of it as a
dagger, a spear, or a two-by-four aimed at the head. Too few
think of it as a gift that can be useful and lead to beneficial long-
term change. The difference may have something to do with our
relationship to the critic, how criticism-tolerant we are, and how
the criticism has been delivered. There are also some people who
cannot handle any criticism, no matter how mild, well presented,
or justified.

Many of us have had positive experiences with criticism delivered lovingly and thoughtfully. Often, however, criticism occurs in
the heat of an argument and, therefore, feels only hurtful. Criticism
used as a weapon in an emotional battle can be damaging to a relationship and it is not easily withdrawn when the battle is over. Many
people dole out criticism with a heavy hand when they are angry or
uncomfortable. Some people store resentments for too long and as
a result deliver their criticism in the form of an explosive discharge,
rather than a thoughtful and gently expressed communication.

When people are unable or unwilling to accept reasonable
criticism, two of the most common—and unfortunate—reactions

are to automatically deny the validity of the criticism, responding with things like "No, I don't," and "That's not true," or to counterattack with "Well, you do it, too," "You're not perfect, either," and "You're crazy."

In improving one's ability to handle criticism, it is helpful to distinguish between the validity of the complaint and how it is expressed. Valid criticism is usually based on accurate perceptions of events or behavior. The critic is motivated by a desire to help and provides solid suggestions for change. Credence should be given to what is being said, particularly if the criticism is expressed by more than one person or if the critic knows a great deal about the subject and is generally someone who has and applies reasonable standards of behavior.

Unjustified criticism may be delivered by someone when you don't live up to his or her expectations. The critic might nag, recite your failures as a person, try to appear smarter or better than you, or criticize what you are doing to get you to do something else. These factors also need to be considered when thinking about the significance of what is being said.

The most useful way to respond to criticism is to show respect for yourself and your critic, without attacking or surrendering. Your intention should be to resolve misunderstandings, acknowledge what may be accurate in the criticism, and reduce the intensity of an unjustified attack.

Three communication techniques that are effective in responding to criticism are acknowledging, disarming, and probing.

Acknowledging: When someone criticizes you and the criticism is accurate, an appropriate response is simply to agree. This technique allows you to accept your mistake without "beating yourself up" or being overly apologetic. Say, "You're right," thank the critic, and apologize or explain yourself, if appropriate. For instance:

Criticism: "Can't you be more careful when you put your dirty clothes in the wash? You left a tissue in your pocket again so now I have to wash everything again!"

Response: "You're right. I should have checked my pockets first. Thanks for washing my clothes again."

Disarming: This is one of the most difficult, yet powerful, techniques for handling criticism. Disarming allows you to respond to the situation without escalating it or acknowledging that you actually agree with how the criticism is expressed.

Criticism: "You're such a slob. You never clean up after yourself."

Response: "You're right. I did leave the dishes in the sink yesterday." (This acknowledges that you left the dishes in the sink, but ignores the exaggeration that you never clean up after yourself and the global judgment that you are a "slob.")

Probing: This technique is effective when you can't tell if the criticism is valid or unjustified because the critic is vague. Probing is a way for you to gain clarification from the critic. Using where, what, when, how, and why questions allows you to elicit the information you need to judge how to respond to the criticism.

Criticism: "You don't work well with the customers."

Response: "Was there a recent situation that concerns you?" Or, "Would you give me an example of what I do that you believe is 'not working well' with the customers?"

Perhaps the very best that one can do when criticism occurs is to recognize it as an opportunity for personal growth. No matter how badly a criticism may hurt, there may be good that can come out of it. Challenging yourself to discover how the criticism can help you is valuable and something to strive for no matter how difficult.

HOW COULD THEY HAVE
SAID THAT?

*Sometimes condolences can hurt
more than they help . . .*

In the course of my nearly four decades as a clinical social work
psychotherapist, I have worked with many patients who have
endured serious illness, suffered a tragic loss, or experienced some
other equally life-altering trauma. In their therapy sessions, many of
them have spoken about the well-meaning friends and relatives who
inadvertently added to their troubles by saying something that was
heard as thoughtless, insensitive, or, at the very least, unsympathetic.

One patient, the mother of two adult daughters, experienced
the anguish of losing her oldest child, who mysteriously died in her
sleep at age twenty-one. At the funeral, a well-meaning neighbor
attempted to comfort her by saying, "Don't feel too bad, you still
have another daughter." Another patient, whose child had died
in utero one month before birth, was told by her obstetrician, "I
don't want you going around feeling like a coffin, okay?" She
hadn't—at least until that remark.

Chemotherapy patients complain about people telling them
how they will or should feel before, during, or after their treatments.
Simple attempts at reassurance, comfort, or support, like "Don't

worry, it'll be okay," or "I'm sure everything will be just fine," are often heard as impersonal and hollow.

A new patient, who recently told me of her attempt to kill herself ten years earlier by jumping out of a window, remembers her therapist predicting that she would soon "forget all about this," as he signed the cast on her broken leg. Another patient, a forty-year-old woman with a terminal illness, was assured by her physician, her lover, and her boss that she would be "just fine."

Comments like these are powerful and often find permanent homes in the memories of their recipients. They often are uttered by individuals described as otherwise sensitive, thoughtful, and supportive. All of us, at times, have felt unsure how best to respond to those in our lives who have undergone a trauma of one kind or another, especially if that trauma was unrelated to our own experience. Our need to provide reassurance or comfort in response to the misfortune of others may lead us to say the very kinds of things described above.

Attempts to "give" to a suffering person may have more to do with our needs than with theirs. The therapist who predicted his patient would "forget" about her suicide attempt may unknowingly have been alleviating his guilt or trivializing this serious event so that *he* could cope with it. The obstetrician's seemingly offhanded advice to his patient may really have been a way of addressing his own feelings about such a tragic loss occurring on his watch. Inadvertently hurtful remarks often come about because of a need to say something, regardless of whether the something we choose has been thoughtfully considered beforehand.

I asked these individuals what they would have preferred to hear from those upon whom they rely for help and support in times of crisis. Generally, they said that reassurance is something they only want from people who know more about their situation than they do. A reassuring comment from a trusted physician, for example, is usually received quite differently than reassuring words from someone who is not really in a position to offer any. They also want people to tell them how they personally feel, (e.g., "I feel terrible for you," or "I'm so sorry") rather than suggest how the sufferer ought to be feeling under the circumstances.

Several patients told me that the words "I'm sorry" have more meaning and value than many of the more elaborate expressions of sympathy and concern they have heard. A patient who recently lost both parents in an automobile accident told me that "as far as I was concerned, there was really nothing to say, so less was more and 'I'm sorry' or 'I'm with you' was just right." Another patient who suffered a miscarriage found little comfort in being told that her loss was God's will working in mysterious ways or that perhaps her fetus was deformed and she should consider herself lucky to have been spared a torturous life. The simple "so sorry for your loss" was the phrase she remembers as being most comforting.

The guidelines that emerge from these troubling stories can be helpful to all of us when we have occasion to comfort or support someone for whom we care:

Think about what you want to say before you say it.

Keep it brief and simple.

Say what you feel and not what you think or wish would be felt by another.

Remember that "I'm sorry" may often be the most helpful thing you can say to someone, regardless of the severity or magnitude of their situation.

➤ See also CANCER OF THE MOOD, following page

CANCER OF THE MOOD

Being patient with ourselves no matter what the circumstances...

M any patients have spoken to me about their experiences with people in their lives wishing that they would—or, worse, telling them that they must—"get over" some emotional condition or disorder from which they are suffering. This could be a state of depression, a grief reaction to the loss of a loved one, or something else that requires time—and maybe professional help—to overcome.

After the terrorist attack on September 11, 2001, I, along with many colleagues in the mental health field in New York City, volunteered to work with individuals and groups of people affected by the tragedy. Some people required months—and longer—to "overcome" the shock and grief associated with losing a loved one. Many felt that there was no such thing as "overcoming" such a loss, but instead looked for whatever relief they could find from the pain and sorrow that troubled them so deeply.

Despite attempts on the part of some professional thinkers and writers to establish timetables and phases for grief reactions, my experience is that grief is a very particular and unique emotional state that every individual experiences differently and it requires varying lengths of time to heal and recover from.

Depression is another emotional state or disorder that sometimes appears to have a life of its own. Often, despite the active
efforts of psychotherapist and depression-sufferer, as well as whatever benefits medication might afford, this mood disorder seems, at
times, to be treatment-resistant and lasts longer than anyone would
have imagined.

Here's the problem: too often, well-meaning friends and relatives
who don't fully understand the plight of the person suffering from
grief or depression will be heard to say things like "What's taking you
so long to get over this?" or "Don't you think you should be better by
now?" or "It's been six months since the funeral, don't you think it's
time to move on?" Many patients have told me that comments like
these simply complicate their grief or their struggle with depression
and make them feel worse, as if they were doing something wrong,
rather than being affected by forces beyond their control. Telling
someone to "snap out of it" when they are consumed with grief or
in the throes of a major depression is not helpful. It lacks understanding and compassion, and does not demonstrate respect for the
obdurate nature of these emotional conditions.

In a discussion with a patient recently, I thought of a possible
way for him to handle the people in his life who were finding his
current depression difficult to tolerate and attempting to be helpful
by "demanding" that he get better. I suggested that if he had a
diagnosis of cancer, as opposed to major depression, and was
receiving chemotherapy, as opposed to psychotherapy and medication, no one would be telling him to "get over it" or "snap out of
it." Rather, they would patiently and hopefully await the results of
the treatment and be supportive and understanding throughout. I
suggested that he explain that he was suffering temporarily from
"cancer of the mood," i.e., depression, and that this explanation

might help well-intentioned family and friends remain supportive without getting impatient and believing that there was more he could and should be doing about his problem.

➤ See also HOW COULD THEY HAVE SAID THAT?, page 79

FORGIVE AND FORGET

Issues that need to be faced when unpardonable events occur...

M any people are under the impression that in order to forgive someone for some offense—like a betrayal, for example—they must somehow forget what happened. These people will sometimes argue that it is impossible to forgive a person for some wrongdoing unless the offending act is somehow exorcised from their system—"deleted from my hard drive," as one patient stated it—or forgotten by some other means.

When forgiveness is somehow linked to a need to forget, the likelihood of achieving the goal of true forgiveness is less likely. We cannot legislate forgetting but it is tempting to view it as a solution to an interpersonal problem. Forgetting may be perceived as a "shortcut" to forgiving; we may imagine that if we could forget about what happened, we wouldn't have to go through the work of forgiving.

There are components of forgiveness that are at times difficult to achieve. We need to feel that the person is truly sorry for the pain they have caused us and that they understand the implications of their actions. It also requires that despite our hurt and anger, we are able to understand how the other could have wronged us. "Forgetting" does not allow these processes to take place. The following are examples of the issues that need to be faced when "unforgivable offenses" take place.

Mindy had arranged for her friend Gil to take care of her dog for her while she was away overnight on a business trip. Gil was to come over to feed and walk the dog the night of her departure and then again in the morning on the day of her return. I'll leave it to your imagination to guess what occurred when Mindy returned and discovered the scene in her apartment as a result of Gil's having forgotten his commitment to do the favor as promised (the dog was okay; the apartment was not). Once her rage over Gil's "unforgivable" offense subsided several days later, Mindy told me that she wanted to try to forgive Gil, her long-time closest friend, since the dog was okay and the apartment had been cleaned up and restored. She asked my help in finding a way to "forget what happened" so that she could forgive Gil and resume their excellent relationship.

Malcolm had a similar belief as Mindy's. For over a decade, he had been urged by family and friends to find a way to forgive his father for a variety of past offenses that led to their complete estrangement. They had been in business together and his father had made a terrible decision that almost led to bankruptcy; a decision, moreover, that he made without consulting his son, which he later agreed was wrong. Nonetheless, this same scenario was repeated later and this time the business was ruined, with legal consequences for both of them.

In a recent session, Malcolm said, "I cannot forgive him because I simply can't forget what he did and the ways he hurt me." It was clear that he was looking for some way to forgive his father, claiming to "want him back, regardless of what he did." He, too, seemed to link the perceived need to forget with the ability to forgive, and clearly was finding it impossible.

Fortunately, both Mindy and Malcolm were helped to achieve the goal of forgiveness once they were able to separate forgiving and forgetting. When they accepted that forgetting the offenses was not likely to happen, they could accept the more viable goal of lessening the negative sensations and ideas that plagued them, so that they could forgive the people they loved and with whom they wanted a continued relationship despite the upsetting events that had occurred. In other words, what happened remains in memory, but becomes much less upsetting and permits the resumption of a relationship with the offending party.

LISTENING PATIENCE

*How to relate to both sides
of your conversation...*

On several occasions, I have observed patients who seemed to be listening when I was talking to them, but left me doubtful about just how much they actually heard. When my doubt is high, I might solicit a response in order to test my impression, since this is obviously important to address. It is my reasonable assumption that if my impression is correct and information presented in therapy is somehow not "getting in," that the same thing is probably going on elsewhere in their lives.

When people who have this difficulty are listening to another speak to them, they are often busy planning how to respond. They might be laying out a defense of their position if a disagreement is involved, or "shutting down" if they are listening to something they don't want to hear. Others may be concentrating on making a favorable impression and, therefore, are busy monitoring the dialogue, rather than hearing it, in order to ensure that they are viewed positively.

Rachel, the wife in a married couple I have been seeing in my practice, is a good example of someone whose apparent listening style concerned me enough to address it directly with her. It was important to do this in a way that was not seen—as much as possible—as blameful or critical so as not to create hurt and, therefore, defeat my effort to help. While observing Rachel listening to her husband recently, I saw that she seemed to be preparing for what she sometimes referred to as "my turn." Ira had said a lot and it was important information that had potential to advance one of their treatment goals. When it was "her turn," Rachel said nothing about anything that Ira had just told her. I asked her if she could tell me—in her own words—what she had just heard. She drew a complete blank and was unable to offer anything. The three of us sat there stunned! The efforts to help Rachel become a more patient listener and to truly focus on what was being said to her have helped her significantly, both in her marriage and in her relationships in general.

Lila, another patient, was a somewhat competitive and combative person who had an argumentative manner of relating to others. "Winning" was quite important to her and this guided her interactions with other people, leading to countless difficulties with family, friends, and coworkers. Early in our work together, I noticed that Lila had trouble waiting to speak, often talking over me or demonstrating impatience when I spoke, however much or little I said. Fortunately, with help and with time, Lila came to appreciate how her manner of relating and what I termed her "listening impatience" were defeating her. In addition to understanding the origins of her particular style of relating, we embarked on an effort to ease the "right/wrong" nature of her interactions and to improve her ability to listen—with good success.

➤ See the following essay for more

MORE LISTENING PATIENCE

*Mirroring and validation—tools for
modifying troubled communication patterns...*

My work with Rachel was in the context of couples therapy
with her and her husband, Ira. With Lila, an individual
patient, the work took place by using our relationship to help her
work things out.

I introduced the concept of mirroring to my patients. Simply
put, mirroring means using "I" language to convey one's thoughts,
feelings, or experiences to the other person in the dialogue. Sham-
ing, blaming, or criticizing the listener is avoided. Instead, the
speaker talks about him or herself. The listener then echoes the
sender's message word for word or by paraphrasing, sometimes
using a lead sentence like, "Let me see if I've got you. You said..."
Mirroring is designed to help a person tune in and carefully listen
to what the other person is really saying, rather than listening to the
reactions and responses going on inside his or her own head. When
Rachel and Ira learned to mirror in this way, their communication
became much more focused and productive. Rather than continue
to recycle their age-old arguments and issues, they began to better
resolve conflicts, settle differences, and generally enjoy their communication because it was no longer as frustrating and contentious.

Validation is another important communications tool that helps people talk to each other more productively and avoid conflict. Validation occurs when each person in a dialogue acknowledges what the other person said, without necessarily agreeing or disagreeing with it. Too often, communication breaks down when a person instantly disagrees with the content, rather than simply acknowledging what was said, i.e., validating the other person. Validation keeps the connection going between the two people in the dialogue, preventing them from getting stuck—often angrily so—in the all-too-familiar "who's right-who's wrong" deadlock. This proved especially helpful to Lila, who too often turned attempts at conversation into contentious exchanges or "debates," as we referred to them, since for her, right and wrong were paramount and she argued her "positions" (all the while complaining that there were fewer and fewer people in her life...perhaps as a result of her communication style). Once Lila benefited from being mirrored and feeling validated, the angry vigor of her argumentative approach to conversing with others was gradually replaced with a more even-tempered and profound level of dialogue with others.

People who did not receive validation in early life are, not surprisingly, the adults who often have the most difficulty with this. Brenda, a patient of mine, is a good example. In the beginning of our therapeutic relationship, Brenda rarely acknowledged anything I said. She would politely listen to my comments and then offer hers. Her remarks, however, were mostly new thoughts or ideas and rarely a direct or relevant response to anything I had just said. Instead of a dialogue, it felt more like a parallel monologue with little, if any, connection between us. When I mirrored her and, in doing so, validated what she had said (i.e., "I hear you, Brenda," "I gotcha," or "That makes sense to me," etc.), our communication improved and enhanced our working alliance immeasurably.

The patient illustrations here represent the effort made on both sides to modify troubled communication patterns that developed over a lifetime and were, therefore, not easily altered. Once some change was realized, however, each patient was able not only to enjoy the improvement, but also to positively influence their communication with others. Mirroring and validation enabled each of them to attain a higher degree of listening patience and a calmer, more thoughtful approach to conversation with others.

➤ See also LISTENING PATIENCE, page 88

DO YOU WANT MY HELP
OR DON'T YOU?

*Acknowledging willingness to help may be
more beneficial than the act itself . . .*

have noticed a curious phenomenon that often creates confusion
in relationships. Sometimes, when people are successful in getting
something they want or need from another, they feel conflicted, perhaps guilty, and they attempt to relieve the other person of whatever
it is they agreed to give. Let me illustrate with the following examples.

Phil was preparing to travel to see his two children who lived
with their mother, his ex-wife, in another city. He wished to have
his new wife, Kim, join him on this particular trip because he anticipated difficulties and wanted her company and support. Kim was
reluctant to go. Phil continued to convince Kim to accompany him
and, after much effort on his part, she agreed. As soon as she said
yes, Phil told her that while he appreciated her willingness to come
with him, it "really was not necessary," he "didn't mind" going
alone. He became adamant about her not going with him, regardless of her willingness to make the trip.

For years, Diane had been after Roy to be more helpful with the
care of their three children and with household chores. She frequently complained about Roy's coming home after work and

behaving more like a guest than a husband and father. Finally, after much work on this issue, Roy began to do more around the house and with the kids, which had a curious effect on Diane. "Oh, honey, you can leave those dishes in the sink. I'll take care of them," she'd say. "You worked hard today, I'll give the kids their baths. It's okay." Understandably, as he expressed it later, Roy was in a quandary. Which message did he listen to? What was the best thing for him to do? Should he let Diane "help" him not to help her—after all these years of pressing him to get more involved?

It appears that some people want to know that an important other person is ready, willing, and able to help, and this is perhaps more important than actually getting the help itself. Phil really did want Kim with him on his trip to see his kids, but felt guilty after she agreed, worrying that he had been overbearing, heavy-handed, and unfair to Kim, none of which he believed or felt about himself when she was initially reluctant to join him. It was as though getting her agreement to go was more important to him than her actually going with him.

Similarly, Diane's long-standing feeling of being unsupported at home by Roy was more about wanting him to be willing to help than it was about the actual help he might provide. Diane felt sorry for "poor Roy" as she watched him perform childcare and household chores and was happy to relieve him of the "burden" she felt she had imposed on him.

These two vignettes illustrate an interesting, yet hard-to-recognize phenomenon; namely, that requests or demands for help or support from those we depend on may have more to do with needing to feel loved and cared for by them. Simply knowing that an important someone is willing and ready to help may be far more important to us than the benefits of the actual help.

SELF-CARE AND THE CARE
OF OTHERS

Beware the double standard of
being caring and attentive to the needs
of others while neglecting yourself . . .

have noticed that many of the patients I have worked with in my
practice seem to be more attentive to the needs of others than to
their own. They behave in caring ways toward their loved ones
while often neglecting their own similar or even identical needs.

I recall the time that I commented to a patient about the elaborate duct-tape repair job he had done on his eyeglasses after having seen this for several weeks. He replied that it "did the job just
fine" and besides, getting new glasses would be "way too expensive." I asked him what he would recommend to his wife or to one
of his children if their glasses had broken. Without missing a beat,
he replied, "Oh, well, I would tell them to go and get new glasses!"
The conversation that followed was interesting and revealing as we
wondered together why it was that he would not want to see them
walk around in tape-repaired eyeglasses any longer than necessary
and why it was that new glasses for them would not be too expensive, but somehow managed to be too expensive for him.

Another patient walked around with painful knees for many months and finally, after some urging from me and others, consulted the appropriate physician. The consultation dragged on for months as I listened to reports of the doctor canceling appointments, not returning phone calls, and even forgetting a scheduled appointment his office had made with my patient—all of which he accepted without question. Meanwhile, I watched him grimace in pain as he got in and out of his chair in my office at each weekly session. Different patient, same question: what would you be doing about this situation if this were a family member's knee problem and not yours? Same answer: "I would never let her tolerate being treated this way by a doctor, and I would not let her walk around in pain for so long without relief!"

These patients, like many others, take considerable pride in their care for their family and friends, and are vigorous in their efforts to seek or provide help for others. Too often, they, of all people, are not on that list...let alone first!

One observation I think may be relevant here is that many people feel their self-esteem is wounded when it comes to their own problems and conditions and the needs that may result, as though having certain needs, especially medical ones, is some form of weakness or personal shortcoming. I see this when patients discuss their own health issues as opposed to the illnesses of others. Some patients, when they happen to be ill, sound apologetic: "I'm so sorry...I *never* get sick." Others are a bit defensive: "I hate to be thought of as a *sick* person. This is just not like me!" Some are even a bit blameful: "My secretary must have given me this lousy cold!" These same people "allow" others to become ill or impaired in some way without judgment or criticism, but not themselves. As a result, going to a healthcare professional, for example, is something they resist or disallow for themselves, even when it is appropriate and necessary.

It seems to me that the wisdom that applies here is rather simple and useful as a guide for action in situations like the ones described above. Beware the double standard of being a caring spouse, parent, and friend while managing to neglect yourself, as though somehow you did not require the same level of care. And, try your best not to be like the doctor in the old *New Yorker* cartoon who counsels his patient about the evils of cigarette smoking while puffing away on one of his own.

BLAMING

*When is it reasonable and appropriate
to point fingers?*

One of the unfortunate ways many people have of addressing a negative situation is to identify the person allegedly responsible for it so that blame can be assigned. I find this to be a most unfortunate impulse, since so many life situations that occur do not require, nor do they benefit from, the identification of a culprit by a blame-focused individual.

Many people report having grown up in a "blaming environment" or a "blame-oriented emotional atmosphere." This suggests a parental or family focus on discovering the culprit involved in a wrongdoing so that he or she can be punished for the transgression committed. There are times, no doubt, when this is necessary and appropriate; occasions where a wrongdoer must be identified and attended to. Examples might include occasions where carelessness leads to a dangerous situation.

There are times, however, when a situation does not require the identification of the offender, particularly when the offense is inconsequential and could be handled by the person discovering the offending act. One patient reported his childhood home atmosphere as one in which any minor infraction—leaving a room without turning off the light, leaving the cap off the toothpaste tube, or forgetting to put a dish in the dishwasher—would lead to a "parental witch hunt" for the responsible culprit. Often, an environment like this one breeds a blame mentality wherein many behaviors are viewed as justifying criticism and punishment.

Blaming is an unfortunate occurrence often observed when working with couples. At times, one member of the relationship is perceived—rightly or wrongly—as "guilty" of some wrongdoing and, therefore, deserving of blame for the alleged offense. One problem with blaming is that it tends to undermine what otherwise might be constructive communication that could lead to better understanding and meaningful change. Another common problem is that the blamer often avoids a necessary self-examination to determine his or her own responsibility for a problem or wrongdoing.

When Paul blamed his wife, Martha, for his extramarital affair with a colleague, he felt justified and managed to absolve himself of any responsibility for his transgression. "It's what guys often do when they're not being satisfied at home," he asserted with self-righteous indignation. The first time he was helped to look at his own responsibility for his behavior was when he was asked to ponder the question of why not everyone chooses to handle that problem by having an affair. The purpose here was not simply to shift blame on the person whose behavior impaired the marriage. It was to have Paul take responsibility for his own actions and not blame Martha, thereby justifying his own unacceptable behavior and absolving himself of any wrongdoing.

With help, Paul was able to examine his motivation for his extramarital affair. He discovered that he had actually used his dissatisfaction in his marriage to justify doing something that he wanted to do anyway and might well have done regardless of whether or not he was or was not a satisfied husband.

Another consequence of what I call a blaming mentality is self-blame, especially when there appears to be little or no justification for it. Many people rush to judgment against themselves without a full examination of the justification for such self-indictment. This propels them into significant emotional distress and often requires professional help.

There are certainly circumstances and occasions when leveling blame at someone else or oneself is fitting and reasonable. One needs to be very careful to differentiate between justifiable and unjustifiable blaming, as well as to have a reasonably forgiving attitude when this may be the appropriate response.

REFUTING COMPLIMENTS

Why can't we just say thank you?

*W*ife: *"Gee, you look cute in that new underwear, honey!"*
Husband: *"No, I don't. I've gained five pounds, I look like a pig, and I'm too flabby!"*

Me: *"It's wonderful that you were able to achieve that, you know!"*
Patient: *"Yeah, well thanks to you and my medication, I was able to."*

Boss: *"Your work has been excellent and we think you've earned the new position of executive assistant, so we're going to move you into that slot next week."*
Office worker (patient): *"Are you sure I deserve it? After all, I'm relatively new here and I don't think I'm that good!"*

New boyfriend: *"I've really enjoyed our relationship and I'm so glad I met you!"*
Patient: *"Oh, you're just saying that."*

I have long wondered why people have so much difficulty accepting compliments and flattering remarks. I have observed this in myself at times, as well. It seems that people have a tendency to repudiate (i.e., reject as untrue) or refute (i.e., prove to be false by arguing or offering evidence) compliments, regarding them as invalid and undeserved. I often wonder why a simple "thank you" is so difficult for so many at moments like these.

I have the impression that many people feel uncomfortable when receiving a compliment because they assume that accepting it outright will be perceived as boastfulness or arrogance. They believe that simple acceptance will appear as though they were too enthusiastically agreeing with the person complimenting them. It would be as if someone told them they looked good and they said, "*Yes!* I sure do!" in response. People would rather appear humble instead of haughty, and one (unfortunate) way to achieve that, it seems, is to refute compliments.

Along with this, some people seem to believe that refuting a compliment is a form of politeness and, therefore, accepting a compliment outright must be impolite. Some variation of denial replaces what would otherwise be appreciation and gratitude for the compliment.

Another reason why people may refute a compliment is because they simply do not believe it's true and thus disavow it. For example, Bob tells Mary that he thinks she's very pretty. Mary responds with such comments as "Oh, no I'm not," or "I'll bet you say that to every woman," or "You must need new glasses." One might imagine that Mary, who has struggled all of her life with a negative self-image, would be pleased to receive Bob's compliment and perhaps even find it reassuring. Instead, she refutes it because his belief about her appearance directly contradicts her own and so Mary has no way to take it in. If she, too, thought she was pretty, she would have been more likely to accept the compliment and be pleased. Unfortunately, this is not the case. In light of Mary's reaction, Bob winds up feeling as if he said something objectionable or problematic when all he did was compliment his girlfriend.

If, for any reason, you are someone who finds yourself struggling with receiving compliments like the people in the examples above, perhaps your own quiet reflection might help you understand why. Rather than expressing yourself in a way that challenges or repudiates a well-intentioned other who seems to have nice things to say about you, a simple "thank you" will always do very nicely while you privately attempt to figure out why a compliment or flattery stirred conflict within you in the first place.

MALADAPTING

*What happens when our attempts
to adapt to a problem intensify
it rather than ease or resolve it?*

In the course of evolution, all species have developed various means and mechanisms to adapt to the conditions that confront them. Some butterflies, for example, assume a protective coloring whereby they so simulate the appearance of the surface on which they rest that they escape detection by their enemies. Certain bird species, unable to find adequate food sources in winter, are able to shrink their stomachs in order to avoid starvation until the spring when food supplies once more become easily available.

Since adaptation is the very essence of life, it is not strange that man, as the most highly advanced species, has developed not only anatomical adjustments, which provide physiological protection in respect to the environment, but also psychological devices, which provide assistance in dealing with emotional needs and life's stresses. These devices help to meet such needs as those for affection, personal security, personal value, and defense against anxiety.

Healthy or "good" adaptation might be exemplified by the person who appropriately adjusts his or her behavior to the requirements and expectations of a new supervisor in the workplace, or by the person who becomes physically disabled and develops new ways of coping and compensating for the loss of a completely healthy body. Another example of "good" or healthy adaptation is the person who suffers the loss of a spouse and eventually adjusts in ways that reflect resilience and excellent coping skills, rather than sinking into extended and disabling depression and despair.

Difficulties arise when efforts to adapt to a new or changed life situation serve to intensify a problem rather than to ease or resolve it. This may lead to what is known as maladapting. There are times when the challenge confronting someone may be to change an external condition or circumstance, rather than adapt to it. In cases like these, "adapting" may actually lead to negative consequences. A woman married to a man who frequently beats her is not someone we want to see adapt to her situation by finding ways to tolerate the abuse and continue living life as a battered wife, for example. Years ago, a patient of mine and several of her female colleagues were being subjected to serious sexual harassment in their workplace. The women developed an informal group that met regularly to discuss and "cope" with the situation they were suffering through together. While this initially appeared to be a good example of adapting to a terrible condition at the office, it turned out to be maladaptive, instead. What these women realized was that by meeting and sharing their common experiences of being sexually harassed by the men in the office, they were comforting each other and learning to live with (i.e., maladapting to) an unacceptable situation. However, they were doing nothing to seek change and put a stop to the horrible conditions they were tolerating and therefore allowing to continue.

There are times when circumstances or conditions in one's life are intolerable and, therefore, not something to which one should adapt. Rather than maladapting by adjusting, tolerating, or enduring unacceptable circumstances or conditions, healthy adapting is sometimes best achieved by changing something.

WELL, IF YOU PUT IT *THAT* WAY...

Being uncomfortable with our aggression can lead to justifying inaction even when we need to address a difficult situation...

One of the interesting things I have observed in my counseling and psychotherapy practice is the way in which some people justify or validate their fears and, therefore, defeat their efforts to make some of the changes they entered therapy to achieve.

This behavior takes many different forms, but there is one type that may be relatively easy to work on if someone is helped to recognize it.

> *Me: "...So what is stopping you from asking him for that raise?"*
> *Caitlin: "I can't just go up to him and say, 'give me more money!'"*

> *Me: "How do you handle it when your roommate eats all your food?"*
> *Judy: "I do nothing, really. If I say, 'why the hell are you stealing my goddamn food,' we'll probably wind up fighting and that would be worse than just losing the food."*
> *Me: "You mean to tell me that he asks to borrow $40 or $50 every week? What do you say when he does that?"*

Frank: "What I want to say is 'who the hell do you think I am, Chase Manhattan?' But it's not me to talk like that, so I say nothing and give him the money."

Me: "So what do you think is preventing you from seeking the divorce you have wanted for so long?"
Ralph: "I just can't go up to her and say, 'I'm outta here!'"

These exchanges illustrate an interesting phenomenon: people who are either afraid of or uncomfortable with their own aggression—like the patients in the above examples—tend to find a way of justifying doing nothing when they genuinely need to handle difficult situations with the people in their lives. In the above examples, the patients involved were expressing their needs or feelings so harshly and unacceptably because that's probably how they believe those comments would sound if they were on the receiving end of them. It's hard to imagine anyone approaching an employer for a raise by saying "give me more money," yet because Caitlin had not imagined any other way of approaching her boss, she avoided making the request for two years, while watching her coworkers seek and obtain salary increases during that time.

Similarly, Judy, a self-described "conflict-avoider," inhibited her reasonable requests and expectations of her roommate in order to maintain a peaceful coexistence. Her angry script for handling the problem ensured that she would remain silent and continue to suffer the consequences of her avoidance. Frank and Ralph's stories were not very different. They, too, constructed angry and unacceptable ways of handling their needs and feelings. As a result, they did nothing.

In each of these instances, the task was to help these patients express their desires in a reasonable way consistent with their values, social judgment, and sense of fairness.

Eventually, Caitlin was able to advocate for her raise in a way that felt right and acceptable and reflected her style of relating to others. Rather than remain a "wimp" by avoiding the issue altogether, Judy, too, found a humorous way of safeguarding her food from her roommate's late-night raids and felt satisfied with her approach.

As long as Ralph had only one way of ending his marriage (to a seriously addicted spouse who refused to seek help), he would never leave. When he developed a thoughtful, sensitive, and caring way of departing, he was able to do so.

The guidelines that emerge from these vignettes can be helpful to all of us when we have occasions to convey difficult, but necessary, information to others. Communicate it in a way that sounds reasonable to you and accept the fact that there are times in our lives when we must ensure that our needs are met even though it might involve discomfort—or even conflict—with others.

DEFENSIVENESS

What does "defensive" actually mean and what activates this response in us?

The following is an example of an exchange between two people—frequently a married couple in a counseling session—that often leads to a troubled stalemate or, worse, intensified frustration and greater conflict. The roles are interchangeable:

> *She: "I hate it when you walk out in the middle of one of our conversations."*
> *He: "I really don't think I do that."*
> *She: "Oh, yes you do!"*
> *He: "NO, I DON'T!"*
> *She: "Don't get defensive!"*
> *He: "I'm NOT being defensive!"*
> *She: "Oh, yes you are."*
> *He: "I'm just disagreeing with you. Stop calling me defensive..."*

When one member of a couple accuses their partner of being defensive, it usually feels like an attack that inspires a counterattack, as most attacks of any kind will do. What gets lost in these exchanges is the issue that was originally raised. Unfortunately, this disenables a meaningful discussion that might have led to deeper understanding and positive behavioral change in both parties. If too often repeated, it also has the effect of creating an atmosphere of despair when two people continually bog down in self-defeating exchanges like this one. Defensiveness is usually a two-way street; when one person becomes defensive, the other person responds defensively and the situation deteriorates from there.

What does "defensive" actually mean and what activates this response in us? Defensiveness is probably best defined as an automatic, emotional response to a perceived threat. It is an unconscious effort to protect the self from anxiety, either through diversionary and intimidation tactics or by distortions of reality. It takes many forms and covers a great many emotionally charged situations. People who are defensive have a tendency to blame circumstances, luck, or others when things don't work out. They create excuses for not having done something, rather than take responsibility. They argue back forcefully in an effort to convince others that they are okay when they sense or know that someone may feel otherwise. Defensiveness exacts a terrible price on relationships. It poisons communication, breeds distrust, and creates roadblocks toward a better understanding of others and ourselves.

Excessive defensiveness may prevent one from learning from his or her mistakes. With a healthy self-esteem, one is able to admit mistakes. However, with low self-esteem, one tends to be too hard on oneself for even small mistakes or overreact and defensively never admit them.

When some people anticipate failing in an attempt at something, they begin telling people why failure is likely. This might apply to a relationship, a new job, or any endeavor where there is uncertainty and outcomes cannot be predicted or guaranteed. This is known as advanced defensiveness and it can increase the likelihood of failure.

Take Liz, for example. She enjoyed both of her dates with Carl, a man she met by chance at a restaurant on her lunch hour. She feared that Carl would not pursue the relationship with her because "He's so wonderful and so smart...why would he want to have a relationship with me?" Liz's subsequent conduct of her relationship with Carl was marked by numerous self-sabotaging behaviors that were designed to help her save face and soften the pain of the rejection that she convinced herself was inevitable. She took days to return phone calls, sounded chilly toward him when they finally spoke to each other, and pretended to be busy when Carl tried to arrange their next date. These were examples of Liz's pattern of protecting a fragile self-esteem and practically inviting the rejection she so dreaded with this very appealing man.

How does someone with a defensive style work to overcome it? There are a few things that might help, but that don't occur easily or without considerable effort. Begin by noticing your feelings, your body, and your words, either expressed outwardly or inwardly, when you feel the urge to defend yourself. By getting to know yourself better, you might be able to discover which responses are working for you and which ones are not. See if it is possible not to feel as though you must always be right or need to prove yourself to others. Rather than become defensive when you feel criticized or imagine a negative outcome of some sort, perhaps you can try to be curious instead, in order to learn something from the feedback you get from others. There is a wonderful sense of freedom when we come to believe that we do not have to defend ourselves in order to prove ourselves, feel understood by another, or be right all the time.

➤ See the following essay for more

MORE THOUGHTS ABOUT DEFENSIVENESS

Techniques for reducing our defensive reactions...

"Stop being so defensive!" is a phrase known to have begun or to have escalated many a battle between people in a relationship. The person told to stop being defensive usually responds by stating that he or she is not being defensive. The accuser then uses that response as evidence to prove his point and an argument ensues. The issue that was the subject of the exchange is lost in the anger storm and not reopened for some time, if ever.

Defensiveness is a term that is used to mean many things. It can refer to someone who blames circumstances, luck, or others when things don't work out, or it can describe someone who creates excuses for not having done something. Defensive people tend to argue back forcefully, get angry when criticized, or feel cornered. Defensiveness is quite common with people who have a fragile self-esteem but also emerges as part of a troublesome dynamic between people who don't know how to resolve conflict effectively.

Patricia and Ken have struggled with a troubled marriage for many years and by the time they entered therapy, they were contemplating divorce. Their arguments had escalated to the point of mutual slander and they could hardly be contained in the treatment room. Each complained that the other was provocative, argumentative, and unable to communicate. "Attack and defend" seemed to be their primary communication style.

Work with this couple was quite challenging and required considerable efforts to help them contain their long-standing mutual resentment and anger. The first step was to help them both be aware of when they were becoming defensive and why, so that they could own it and use their self-awareness in constructive ways. Defensiveness blocks our ability to take in feedback from others, so it is important to recognize defensive behavior in ourselves, not just in others. When both Patricia and Ken were at the point where each could identify their own defensiveness, the anger level in their relationship diminished considerably. Their new self-awareness was celebrated by both as a significant achievement and deservedly so.

Improving one's ability to listen to others and truly hear what is being said is another important way to reduce defensiveness. Since defensive responses occur so spontaneously, it is important to slow down in interactions with others so that there is time to process what is occurring and then respond in more positive and less defensive ways. Patricia, both in and out of her relationship with Ken, was notorious for what I call defensive preemptive strikes. Fearing failure or defeat, she would declare its likelihood before it occurred. When Patricia told Ken that she would lose their tennis match before they even started to play, for example, she was attempting to protect herself and get relief from her anticipated failure. The belief that she would lose may actually have increased the likelihood that she would do so. In addition, it detracted from the pleasure and enjoyment of what was supposed to be a casual athletic and social encounter with her husband.

Ken struggled with self-doubts about his intelligence for years and, as a result, tended to become defensive when he imagined his intelligence was being questioned or doubted by another. This might explain why when Patricia once told him in a therapy session that she didn't think he understood what she meant, Ken had a defensive reaction, saying, "What do you think I am, stupid?" A nondefensive response might have sounded something like, "Okay, then help me understand," or "What is it I'm missing?" By responding nondefensively, rather than closing himself off in anger, he might have learned something from Patricia.

One of the best ways to limit or reduce your own defensive reactions—in addition to becoming more aware of them—is to challenge the ways in which you are self-critical. When you have a tendency to be self-critical and disparage yourself for your weaknesses, limitations, or failures, you are more likely to become defensive when you perceive others—rightly or wrongly—thinking the same way about you. Working this out, i.e., striving to become more self-accepting and tolerant of your limitations and vulnerabilities, is the key to achieving a much less defensive self.

Loving

Our Partnered Relationships

SOME THOUGHTS ON WHAT MAKES A RELATIONSHIP SUCCESSFUL

The ingredients for a positive and successful romantic partnership...

I t is distressing when a patient tells me that they have never observed—or experienced—what they would define as a successful romantic relationship. Statements like "Maybe good relationships just don't exist" or "No one in my family ever had a good relationship" usually follow. Many patients enter psychotherapy because of relationship-based difficulties and some of them eventually feel that they are doomed to continuously have trouble or fail in their efforts to enjoy a successful romantic partnership.

I am often told by clearly disheartened patients that the trajectory of their romantic lives has been downhill. Frustrations and disappointments are said to develop as early as a few years—sometimes even a few months—after the honeymoon ends and "normal life" resumes. One patient told me that he and his wife suffered from the marital equivalent of a "postpartum depression that never ended." Frequently, in order to comfort themselves, it seems, they suggest that this downward trajectory is "standard," and "everyone's experience." These assertions, I fear, while primarily designed to self-soothe, also seem to firm up the belief that any long-term romantic relationship is likely to be a doomed enterprise. When I comment that while relationships may change over time and that change does not necessarily imply that a relationship turns from positive to negative, or when I mention that some relationships have been known to deepen and improve with age, some patients looked at me in disbelief.

Through my work, I have had the satisfaction of seeing positive outcomes when two people work hard at relationship self-improvement. This enables me to work with a perspective and a conviction about what may be possible that patients in distress—especially in the beginning of the therapeutic process—often lack.

The following are some of the ingredients that I believe help to make and sustain a positive and successful romantic partnership:

Handling anger and avoiding arguments: One of the major problems with anger and the arguments that result is that neither partner does much, if anything, to avoid them. Perhaps motivated by the need to prevail or be "right" about the conflict-arousing issue, one or the other person in the couple "takes the bait" and gets hooked into an argument that could have been avoided if one of them had seen to it that the conversation—however emotionally charged—had remained conversational or been postponed until calm was restored. This is not always easy, but certainly possible.

Listening to each other: This is extremely important. Couples in conflict are often so busy preparing their indictment of the other person or their defense of themselves that they simply do not listen and hear what is being said. Thus, their responses are often not responses at all, but their next statement—perhaps entirely unrelated to what was just said to them. This is one of the main reasons, I believe, why too many couples recycle the same issues and arguments repeatedly and rarely if ever feel as though any conversation (or "attack and defend" exchange) accomplishes anything. Couples often need help to learn to listen to each other so that the dynamic between them changes to one that is productive. That is the job of good therapy.

Saying "I'm sorry": I continue to be amazed at how difficult this is for so many of the people with whom I have worked, both in and out of romantic partnerships. I often hear statements like, "I know it's the right thing to do and I feel sorry...I just can't say it!" Such responses suggest the likelihood that the person might feel "weak" or "defeated" if they publicly acknowledge their sorrow or regret.

Expressing Gratitude: When partners in a couple feel and express gratitude or appreciation for each other, each of them feels cherished and valued and it enhances the relationship. Expressions of appreciation do not have to be confined to major gestures or actions. "Thank you, honey, for feeding the dog" or "I really appreciate your picking up my prescription" can be just as meaningful as a thank you for a monumental gift or kindness.

Changing: Yes, changing, and by this I am referring to what might be considered the "little things" that become big when they persist over time. These are the kinds of changes that, with some effort, might be easy to accomplish and have far greater dividends than the investment required to achieve them. If a wife tells her husband, for example, that she really appreciates getting a greeting card on her birthday and her anniversary, I am bewildered by the husband's seeming refusal to gratify her, regardless of whether or not it means anything to him. If a husband informs his wife that he would like not to be interrupted by phone calls while at his gym workout unless there is an emergency, I am similarly bewildered by her not cooperating by calling about nonessential matters during that time. When people feel ignored or, worse, devalued by their partners, resentments develop that can become toxic to the relationship.

Treating each other as special: A wife once complained that upon leaving a party, her husband helped every other woman guest on with her coat—except her. When she questioned him about this, his reply was "Well, that's because you're my wife!" Her response: "That's the point!" That she felt taken for granted was not surprising. Moments like this may be insignificant if they are infrequent, but if they typify an attitude or are common in the relationship, they have the potential to cause diminished regard and affection for the offending partner.

Hurting with words: The damage potential of comments made in the heat of battle is extremely high. There is a tendency on the part of the offending partner to dismiss or trivialize those remarks afterward. Saying "I didn't really mean it, I was just angry," often makes things worse, especially if there is no sincere apology attached. Words can cause wounds that may not easily heal when calm is restored. They are often referenced when a subsequent argument occurs, i.e., "I'll never forget the time you told me to 'drop dead.'"

These are but a few of what might be considered "ingredients" of a successful romantic relationship—and, perhaps, any relationship, especially ones that involve conflict. Every one of these ingredients is best utilized by both partners when, above all else, they remember that the person with whom they are having conflict may be the very person whom they love the most and who loves them the same way.

➤ See also SAYING 'I'M SORRY,' page 147

CHRONIC COUPLES CONFLICT

What causes our disagreements?

When most couples call me for a couples therapy consultation, they are at a point where the severity of their ongoing conflict has reached the danger zone. Some couples seek help when the early signs of trouble begin to develop. Others wait... and wait, hoping either that their difficulties will resolve themselves or that they will find a way to address their problems independent of professional help. Some couples, it seems, choose to consult a therapist as the "option of last resort" before initiating divorce proceedings.

When I see a new couple for the initial consultation, I am particularly interested to learn how they are—or are not—able to resolve conflicts, often the primary issue in their marital disharmony. There are couples who have been recycling the same conflicts for months, even years, often resulting in erosion of affection or, worse, loss of love for each other. Why does this happen?

There are several reasons, I believe, that lead to conflict between couples. They include an inability or unwillingness to listen, readiness to anger, the need to "win" arguments, and an inability or unwillingness to apologize.

Inability or unwillingness to listen: In the throes of conflict, people have a tendency to become preoccupied with their position and get very busy finding ways to "sell" it to the other person. Vigorous persuasion or, worse, verbal bludgeoning of the other takes place. In addition to the unfortunate consequences of this approach, it is most probable that listening—real listening, in order to learn what the other person is thinking and feeling—is unlikely. In conflict, people often talk over each other and are, therefore, only hearing themselves and not the other. This is why couples therapists sometimes feel like referees. Real listening, which requires maturity, impulse control, healthy restraint, and respect for the other person in the exchange, is vitally necessary, but too often difficult to achieve.

Readiness to anger: Whether or not a particular individual has a problem with managing their anger, this emotion too often plays a role when couples attempt to address their differences. Some people are simply unable to tolerate differences of belief, opinion, or approach to an issue in the relationship and feel betrayed, disregarded, or somehow diminished when differences of any kind come to the surface. Some people see devotion and loyalty as requiring agreement or conformity, even submission, and when this is not readily offered by their partner, they become angry and less likely to engage in rational effort to reconcile differences where this is necessary and appropriate.

Need to "win" arguments: The common expression "win the battle, but lose the war" applies here. Certain individuals, perhaps those with strong competitive tendencies, seem more concerned with victory in an argument than with how the relationship fared in the course of the dispute. Relationships accrue damage over time when too many arguments end with a winner and a loser or when a person feels overwhelmed by the contentious force of their partner. This often leads to resentment that might be stored and provide material for the next conflict.

Inability or unwillingness to apologize: This, in my view, is a major problem in some relationships, since too often it causes conflicts to remain unresolved and leads to "repeat performances," i.e., the argumentative replaying of certain issues that become chronic areas of difficulty between partners. There is rarely value for a couple in finding themselves re-arguing the same issue many times over, especially when a sincere and heartfelt apology by either or both partners might have helped them to move on and success-fully restore their positive alliance. Heartfelt apologies can re-stabi-lize the couple, moving them out of their state of conflict to a prior experience of closeness.

These causes of conflict in couples, while certainly not a com-plete list, do highlight some of the typical struggles that many cou-ples undergo.

MIXED SIGNALS

Making sense of things that don't add up...

Emily was excited after her blind date with Walt. More than any man she had met in years, he was charming, funny, successful, and seemed as taken with her as she was with him. They had much in common and both indicated their pleasure in finally meeting someone with whom they wished to spend more than twenty minutes. After a polite first kiss in the lobby of her apartment building, he promised to call within a few days to arrange their next date. That was the last Emily ever heard from Walt.

Bruce had a similar experience. Following a spirited and flirtatious encounter with Melissa on a business trip, he called to arrange the dinner date they had discussed having the next week. Six days and four unreturned phone calls later, he gave up, feeling defeated and confused by Melissa's unresponsiveness.

Both Emily and Bruce attempted to do what most of us do when life hands us mysteries like the ones described above—they tried to make sense of something that made no sense to them at all. Their attempts to solve the mystery of their disappointing romantic experiences revealed a great deal about them. Emily, a successful business entrepreneur with a solid sense of herself, is a positive thinker, an optimist by nature, and someone who reasons things out in a thoughtful and rational manner. She reacted to Walt's behavior with a mixture of bewilderment and disdain for his failure to follow through as promised. She felt that it was "his loss," that perhaps he was—for reasons that were unclear—afraid to pursue a romantic partnership with her, had problems with intimacy, or simply was not mature enough to handle himself any better than he did.

Bruce's effort to make sense of his mystery was characterized by his feelings of inadequacy, his tendency to be self-critical, and his unfortunate belief that he was a less-than-appealing romantic partner, especially to women to whom he felt an attraction. Unlike Emily, Bruce was devastated by the way in which he was treated by Melissa, feeling deeply wounded by her rejection.

The guidelines that emerge from these stories are as follows: Accept that some things cannot be explained, especially since we cannot read the minds of others. Beware a tendency to fill in the blanks by referencing yourself, especially negatively. Finally, accept the fact that disappointment and rejection happen to everyone, not just to you.

➤ See also DEFENSIVENESS, page 110
         MORE THOUGHTS ABOUT DEFENSIVENESS,
         page 113

WHEN INTIMACY BREEDS CONFLICT

How much is too much?

For some people, intimacy is a challenge and a source of considerable concern. For others, it feels like a language in which they are fluent and, therefore, can easily converse. Many people worry—perhaps deservedly, perhaps not—about their capacity for intimacy, especially if they have been labeled as being somehow intimacy-deficient.

Most experts would agree that the ability to have intimate relationships is a highly desirable quality. Researchers in this area have offered evidence to suggest that people who score high on various intimacy scales and questionnaires demonstrate other desirable qualities. These individuals seem to engage in more intimate behaviors, they disclose more about themselves to others, they feel more in control of their fate, they tend to be more active, and they experience less alienation from friends, family, and self.

Problems with intimacy seem often to be related to how different people define intimacy and how they handle the intimacy-related issues that emerge in their important relationships.

During the early phase of their couples therapy, Martha claimed that Phil was not able to be adequately intimate, while Phil claimed that he had no problem whatsoever with intimacy. His problem, he claimed, was that Martha was never satisfied with his many efforts at being an intimate spouse. Martha complained that Phil never said "I love you," suggesting to her that he had "problems with intimacy." Phil replied, "For the past three years, I have driven six miles out of my way on Fridays after work to buy you those special pickles you love so much. Doesn't that sound like love to you?"

Going out of his way to buy a favorite food for his wife was Phil's way of expressing his intimate feelings for her. Martha, because of her different criteria, saw his weekly gesture not as loving, but as dutiful behavior on the part of a cooperative spouse. For her, Phil had a problem with intimacy, while Phil felt his means of expressing intimacy were being devalued.

Sometimes intimacy takes unconventional forms. The adult children of an older couple once referred their parents to me because of concerns about their constant arguing. The couple reluctantly attended the first session and quickly began to do what they had been doing for the entire forty-five years of their marriage: argue. The "conflict-ridden" marriage I had been asked to "treat" turned out to be a stable, intact, secure relationship that showed no signs of falling apart, as their children feared. It seemed to me I was watching two reasonably happy people for whom arguing represented a form of intimacy both were comfortable with—even though no one else was.

While it is certainly desirable to have a high degree of intimacy with one's partner, it's also important to be clear about how one defines and understands various forms of intimate behavior.

IS DEPENDENCY UNHEALTHY?

*Contrasting dependency levels can
impair relationships...*

For many, the term "dependency" connotes weakness and an inability or unwillingness to rely on oneself. It is a term often used interchangeably with the word "needy," which, most would agree, is not generally used in a positive or complimentary way. Others see their dependency needs as a healthy part of their attachment to cherished loved ones upon whom they rely and whose reliance upon them they welcome.

This issue can be a hot button between men and women who often have very different ideas about dependence and independence. These differences in their comfort with feelings of dependency are common and do not necessarily reflect how much one person cares about the other. When these differences are not clarified between the two people in a relationship, hurt feelings and misunderstandings may result, leading some couples into counseling.

Whenever Steve had an important decision to make, he tended to ponder in silence until he figured out what he wanted to do. He would then share the results with Emily, his wife, who frequently felt left out of the process and believed that Steve did not trust her enough to depend on her input. Emily had a very different style and a different need than Steve. For her, important decisions often involved surveying close friends and relatives, especially Steve, until she collected enough information to figure out what to do.

Similarly, when Steve became ill, he preferred to be left alone until he fully recovered. He did not seek, nor did he particularly appreciate, Emily's frequent expressions of concern and offers to help. When she became ill, she wanted nothing more than for Steve to spend hours at her bedside offering tea and sympathy. Steve and Emily's dependency needs, while different, seem to be "variations of the norm," i.e., preferences and acceptable differences between people who understand and adjust to their partner's needs without much difficulty.

Problems occur when differences in a couple's dependency needs are extreme or when one or both partners suffer from a dependency disorder. People who have excessive dependency needs tend to have difficulty making everyday decisions without a great deal of advice and reassurance from others. They also avoid conflict because they fear losing the support and approval of important people in their lives. They may worry about being able to care for themselves and, therefore, desperately seek a new attachment as a replacement for a lost relationship. We all know people who are unable to disengage from a romantic partner if it means they will have to be alone for a while. They tend to leave someone only when they are newly involved in a replacement relationship so their dependency needs will be met continuously.

Life together will be easier for people with similar dependency needs and styles. However, differences between partners in these ways should not be mistaken for different levels of caring.

MARRIAGE IS A VERB, NOT A NOUN

Why do our relationships become something less, instead of something more?

Many years ago, I was asked to lead a workshop on a topic of my choice and decided to give a talk and lead a discussion on the subject of "Marriage is a verb, not a noun." As you can probably guess, the gist of the presentation was that marriage is an "action" word, an action experience—or should be if it is not already. The idea resonated with many people and my workshop enjoyed a standing-room-only audience and an enthusiastic response. I remember several people commenting on the many divorces in their families and among their friends. They were coming for help to ensure that they would not wind up among them.

One of the most common complaints heard from romantic partners, whether married or not, is that they no longer feel the excitement, the intrigue, the joy, which, they claim, has waned or even evaporated. This may be especially true for those who are well into the years of the marital adventure, but there are also those who sing a very different tune. Romantic partners in this category speak of the deepening of their relationship, the way it has "aged like an excellent wine" or become even more interesting and multi-dimensional than it was when they married in their twenties or thirties.

There are many ways to understand the differences in their experiences. Such things as family history (certainly including the nature and quality of their parents' marriage), ability to relate to others, character type, capacity for handling conflict, and the overall quality of the marriage are all involved in understanding why for some the marital experience has been a somewhat dull or downhill ride, while for others it is the central joy and main journey in their lives.

There are several possible explanations for why the relationship might have become something less, instead of something more, over time. One might concern the extent to which a romantic partner feels that they are no longer getting their needs met in the relationship, so they may have stopped investing in it. This response can certainly signal trouble since the disinvestment is often indirect, subtle, and unspoken, so it tends to stimulate similar withdrawal behaviors on the part of the relationship's other partner.

Another explanation might be what happens to couples "when the novelty wears off." This, for some, might take years; for others, it can happen on the honeymoon or even before! The way to avoid this relationship development, of course, is to make sure that efforts are made by both parties to keep the relationship fresh and exciting, rather than watch it wilt and be allowed to feel like a comfortable, but hardly used, old shoe that no longer gets polished. This is consistent with the notion that a marriage or any important relationship is something you do, i.e., a verb, rather than something you have, i.e., a noun.

➤ See also MARITAL DATING, following page

MARITAL DATING

How can we keep our relationship from becoming a routine?

n my ongoing work with couples, I have often listened to stories from patients about unfortunate developments in their relationship. They sound something like this: "We just don't have fun anymore." "This marriage has been in a rut since our firstborn came along." "There's no romance left." "We're like a pair of comfortable old shoes...don't wear 'em much, but don't wanna throw 'em out, either." "Intimacy? Are you kidding? What's that?"

When I think it's appropriate and the timing is right, I have introduced the idea of marital dating and have marveled at some of their reactions. "That's a better oxymoron than 'jumbo shrimp!'" "Hey, Dr. J., you must have gone to therapy school on Pluto...couldn't have been this planet!" "That's funny! Got any more good jokes?"

With these couples, once we get beyond the shock and the humor, a serious exploration of the idea often occurs. Some patients are intrigued by the possibility of reactivating the spirit of their courtship and consider having what one couple called "a revival." It is always interesting to observe the excitement as two people begin to imagine what "dating" might consist of at this point in their relationship. (Such marital dating discussions have been conducted with couples who have been together for as long as thirty-eight years and for as short a time as one year.)

Almost always, especially in the first or second session with a new couple, I ask each one to tell me the story of how they met and describe the courtship experience. Most often, the previously gloomy and upsetting statement of the reasons why they came to see me is replaced by positive interaction, laughter, and simple joy at how wonderful things used to be. Some people have thanked me for asking about this since they had "forgotten" what it once was like and had not visited that place and time in their lives for quite a while. Clearly, the "new normal" had become their relationship troubles; the earlier positives and satisfactions were long gone from memory.

The idea of marital dating is consistent with the idea, explored in the previous essay, that "marriage is a verb, not a noun," and with the distinction discussed earlier between problems and conditions. For example, if a couple sees their sluggish or unfulfilling relationship as a condition, they are more likely to accept it as such, do nothing about it, and muddle through. If, on the other hand, a couple views their less-than-satisfactory relationship as a problem, then they are much more likely to work to solve it since, as we know, a problem is something we try to solve; a condition is something we live with.

Once a couple embraces the idea of dating as a viable relationship activity, the ways in which they approach this are, essentially, up to them and something they often have fun working out. One couple had a regular date immediately following their weekly couples session. Another couple's date was their weekly dinner and dance lesson. A third couple handled this by taking turns surprising the other with a "mystery date" every Friday after finding a babysitter for the first time in six years!

There is a wonderful *New Yorker* cartoon with an older couple sitting in front of a marriage counselor. The husband says to the counselor, "No heavy lifting!" As a couples counselor, I am always pleased when the introduction of a simple idea like "marital dating" inspires a couple to do the "heavy lifting" all by themselves.

➤ See also MARRIAGE IS A VERB, NOT A NOUN, page 133, PROBLEM OR CONDITION?, page 171

AMBIVALATIONSHIPS

Why do some people who seek long-term relationships resist commitment?

Many people are quite clear about their desire for a romantic partnership that has a future. For some, it is a great need that represents an all-consuming endeavor that occupies a good deal of their time and energy. Some others are more casual about it and would like a romantic partner, but treat the matter as a desirable life option that may or may not occur. Still others are clearly not interested in a single partnership that might lead to permanence. They prefer their single status and live life accordingly.

Problems arise for certain individuals—and the people they invite or allow into their lives—when they are unsure or confused about their needs. They often send mixed messages to the people with whom they develop a relationship. Interestingly, they tend to find partners who seem to accept their ambivalence, rather than demand clarity and relationship definition early on.

Cynthia and her long-term boyfriend Eddie began dating in 2004 and moved in together in 2006. Cynthia, now thirty-five years old, has long assumed that she and Eddie would be together permanently, get married at some point, and eventually have a family. Eddie, it seems, was quite comfortable with the existing arrangement and, despite occasional comments about their future together, showed little sign of wishing to advance the relationship beyond its current state. When Cynthia began to feel concerned about their union, she discovered that while she wanted a husband, Eddie was quite content to have what we termed a "permanent girlfriend."

Similarly, Ruth and James have been together for four years and are treated—and treat themselves—like an "old married couple," except for the fact that they are not, in fact, married, and the topic of marriage is a hot-button issue for them. James, age forty-five, has never been married, but is eager to become Ruth's husband. Ruth, twice divorced and a wary soul, is reluctant to "do this again" for fear that this marriage might "wind up like the first two" and be a "third failure." She encourages James to remain interested in the possibility of eventual marriage as the natural destination of their relationship, but she tends to resist his efforts to discuss the subject, let alone make specific plans to secure their future together. James often says, "I love you and I want to be with you forever." Ruth tends to respond with comments like "Isn't what we have good as is? Why tamper with success by getting married? Why don't we just leave well enough alone?"

Both Eddie and Ruth are in what I call "ambivalationships." They want the relationship, seem to want it to remain permanent, act and feel like the other half of a typical marital relationship, yet resist the conventional route that long-term couples generally travel, i.e., marriage. By many measures, there is nothing inherently wrong with these relationships and others like them, save for the fact that they involve a power imbalance between the two people involved that eventually creates a crisis or simply erodes the health and welfare of the partnership.

Cynthia and James, both of whom are obviously interested in permanence via marriage, are basically powerless to influence change in their respective partners unless by, perhaps, putting the relationship on probation or just ending it, something they are loathe to do. Eddie and Ruth, by virtue of their ambivalence about permanence via marriage, have the power to determine what happens next, something that often leads to anger and resentment on the part of the waiting partner.

Clearly, it is helpful, respectful, considerate, even humane for someone in a significant long-term relationship to resolve any ambivalence they have about changing the status of that relationship, especially when they are well aware of the wishes and feelings of their partner. Too many romantic partnerships linger in a state of uncertainty with one member of the couple living ambivalently while resisting or avoiding discussions about the future when these arise. Both parties have the responsibility, it seems to me, to see to it that the state and fate of their union is handled openly and honestly, leading to mutual understanding and resolution.

ANGER AND COUPLES

How can we use anger to strengthen communication and enhance our relationships?

Throughout my years of providing counseling and psychotherapy to patients, I have had the opportunity to work with many couples that have sought help for a variety of reasons and needs. Like any therapist who sees couples, the hope is always that both the timing of their seeking help and the nature of their presenting problems affords an opportunity for meaningful work and significant benefit.

Many couples, unfortunately, wait to seek help until it is the last stop before the lawyer's office. Some, in fact, come to therapy having already made contact with an attorney to explore separation and divorce. Often, but certainly not always, this might make marital treatment a "too little too late" experience for one or both parties. Other couples might contact a therapist at the first signs of early difficulty in their relationship, when one or both realize that the time to address the issues is sooner, rather than later, before destructive patterns of relating become entrenched and, therefore, harder to modify.

Working with couples has always been challenging and a fascinating laboratory in which to observe and participate in the complex dynamic of two often very different people trying to work out differences and develop greater closeness in an effort to restore a once-healthier relationship.

Many couples new to marital therapy are on their best behavior, perhaps because they are not yet comfortable enough to demonstrate the nature of their troubled relationship in front of a relative stranger. Other couples treat the therapist's office like their own living room and within minutes show me just how terrible things between them have become. Either is fine and affords a way of getting to know both parties to begin to figure out how to help them.

Not surprisingly, anger is quite a common emotion in couples work, but the degree to which it exists, the ways in which it gets expressed, and the ability of an angry partner to control or contain his or her anger become central to the quality of the therapeutic work that lies ahead. Couples will often raise important issues in a session in the hope of achieving a new and better understanding of themselves and their partners. Many of the issues, understandably, involve disagreement and possible conflict, as a result. Partners often need a forum in which to work things out with each other and the therapist's office frequently works better—at least for a while—than the living room or bedroom at home.

Problems become compounded when one or both partners are so angry at each other and have so much difficulty containing and channeling their anger that reasonable, rational, and loving—yes, loving—conversation is disenabled. Often, when anger shows up in an important, emotionally charged conversation, the conversation abruptly shifts and becomes all about the anger. This is one of the main reasons why many couples may not achieve the important treatment goals they agreed to work toward in their couples therapy.

The message is this: in your relationship with your partner (with anyone, for that matter), make sure that if and when you become angry, you use the anger to strengthen your communication and accomplish something that benefits the relationship. Avoid causing damage, possibly irreparable, to a relationship by losing control of yourself and using your anger as a "weapon of mass destruction." Remember, too, especially in the case of relating to your romantic partner, that you are communicating with someone you love and who loves you. Hopefully, that realization alone will help you to avoid saying something harmful and regrettable and enable you to work productively together toward a much-improved partnership.

AM I DATING OR AM I IN A RELATIONSHIP?

A small shift in thinking can result in a big change when it comes to our partners . . .

George, a fifty-five-year-old executive who's been divorced for two years, has been dating two women he met through an Internet matchmaking service. The two new associations were in varying stages of development and George was enjoying the experience of "comparison shopping" before deciding which one of the two would, hopefully, become his "one and only" and eventually, perhaps, his second wife.

He had informed both women that he was seeing someone else besides them and had been positively handling the occasional complications of dating more than one person at a time. While there were clearly some benefits in having two dating options, George was seriously interested in clarifying his interests and intentions and having a full relationship with one of the women as soon as possible.

Neal, a physician in his late forties, was having quite a different experience. Neal was in the fourth year of his divorce from a woman to whom he had been married for twenty-five years. He, like George, was dating two women, but, unlike George, was feeling conflicted and guilty and having difficulty enjoying his time with either woman, seemingly because of the very existence of the other. He suffered from the nagging belief that somehow or other he was doing something wrong by dating two women at the same time.

Having these two men as patients in my practice at the same time afforded me an opportunity to learn something about the ways different people handle the experience of dating, especially when there are multiple partners. Several interesting and challenging issues emerged as the work with both men progressed.

My sessions with Neal focused on his intense discomfort about feeling that somehow he was "betraying" both women by dating them simultaneously and choosing not to inform either one about the existence of the other. Invited to consider letting both dating partners know that he was not seeing them exclusively felt premature and presumptuous to Neal, since both involvements were in their early stages. He was reluctant to assume or inadvertently encourage exclusivity with either woman.

What was discovered during the course of exploratory work with both men was that a key reason why George seemed conflict-free while Neal was so conflict-ridden was traceable to the way in which each one defined his particular experience. George was dating and, by his definition, would continue doing so with as many women as he pleased until he chose one and then entered into a relationship. For him, dating was associated with "freedom," "exploration," "evaluation," and "discovery." What Neal and I discovered about his conflict was that his definition of dating was a first-encounter-only experience, so that as soon as he saw a woman for the second time, he was in a relationship, which, for him, was quite different from dating and was associated with "commitment," "loyalty," "devotion," and "exclusivity." No wonder Neal was in such conflict. While it is possible to date two women concurrently, it is not okay to be having two relationships at the same time, which is the real reason, we learned, why he did not want to reveal each woman's existence to the other and why he felt that he was "betraying" and "cheating on" two women he cared about and did not wish to hurt in any way.

Sometimes a seemingly simple and obvious insight like the one I've just described is all that is necessary to help someone feel better and be able to determine a suitable course of action that can lead to personal growth and meaningful change.

SAYING "I'M SORRY"

Apologizing can be a difficult thing to do, but the rewards often make it worth the effort . . .

I have often observed in my work with patients, especially with couples, something that continues to baffle and cause concern: the inability to say "I'm sorry." On many occasions, I have heard reports of a conflict with someone in considerable detail. Often, a patient will acknowledge that he or she was responsible—partially, if not completely—for an unfortunate experience with a partner, friend, or colleague, for example. I listen for evidence of regret and remorse when I believe that to be an appropriate response based on the details of the story. Typically, there are three conclusions to stories like these.

One response involves the virtual absence of responsibility for the conflict and the belief that the other person is completely at fault and, therefore, no apology is necessary. Another is the complete or partial acceptance of personal responsibility, accompanied by an apology to the offended party. The last is when someone is able to acknowledge responsibility, but either will not or cannot bring themselves to offer an apology. This third response is the one that interests me.

Many people, it seems, experience apologizing as a sign of weakness. Interestingly, when asked if they view it that way when the apology comes from another, they do not see it as weakness at all, but rather the "right" or "responsible" thing to do. Remarkably, some will say it is a sign of strength or maturity when the apology is offered by the other person, but still feel that it is an unacceptable admission of defeat—or weakness—when the apology is theirs to give to someone else. Interesting, don't you think?

During couples counseling, often I will hear reports of a terrible argument or fight that occurred outside the session. I will hear statements of sorrow about things said in the heat of battle or deep remorse about the possible relationship damage caused by hateful words or even worse behavior. At some point, I might ask the offending party whether he or she apologized and too often, it seems, the response is no.

Another reason why people fail to apologize is not because they are trying to be rude or mean, but because they just are not used to saying it. Perhaps they might have difficulty with recognizing apology-worthy situations. Perhaps they do not appreciate the value of an apology, especially to a loved one. Perhaps it is simply not part of their interpersonal repertoire. I have often witnessed anger evaporate, resentment disappear, and coldness toward another melt before my eyes when a clearly heartfelt "I'm sorry" is offered. An apology given reluctantly, insincerely, or with resentment has the potential to make matters worse and is best avoided.

"I'M REALLY GLAD WE HAD THIS TALK"

How can we feel better after an emotionally charged conversation instead of worse?

One of the major issues confronting so many couples is what is commonly referred to as communication problems. This can mean many things and may cover a wide variety of interactive difficulties between any two people in a relationship.

One of the things I hear repeatedly from my patients is that controversial topics in the relationship are completely avoided on the assumption that to do so may be better than to "fight." Often, and unfortunately, it seems that fighting may indeed have been the only other alternative in their relationship experiences. One self-proclaimed "relationship sufferer" complained that her intended discussions with her husband immediately turned into "attack and defend" exchanges. Each partner focused on leveling criticisms and then defending or justifying their positions to each other, thereby making their so-called communication a negative experience. This level of exchange is likely to produce two people who will be inclined to avoid talking about issues that arise between them, possibly leading to the erosion or deterioration of their relationship.

Another problem occurs when one or both partners in a relationship are prone to intense anger when they feel misunderstood, misperceived, or even just disagreed with, because they have a strong need to be "right" or have their view or idea accepted by the other. Among other damages, this type of interaction forces their attention to the anger itself and its various harmful consequences, including increased hurt, distance, and withdrawal, and away from the issue at hand, which then may never be discussed again, much less satisfactorily resolved.

For several of the above reasons, many couples wind up recycling the same arguments (as opposed to discussions) and, therefore, dread the next encounter when their partner wants or needs to talk about something. Some couples have told me that they have been having essentially the same argument for years with no movement whatsoever. In one instance, the topic of the multi-year dialogue was their poor communication and what to do about it!

Mike and Adrienne needed to deal with an important conflict about which they each had strong feelings and major differences. Their friends Dave and Mara were coming for dinner and Adrienne was unhappy to be hosting them due to Dave's alcoholism and his verbally abusive treatment of his wife. Mike liked them both and was more tolerant and accepting of Dave's behavior, though not at all approving. Before their friends' arrival, Mike and Adrienne absented themselves for a while to talk in private and see whether they could settle things between them.

Later that day, Mike told me about the talk that he and Adrienne had had, which evidently was quite productive and enabled them to receive their guests with a different attitude and level of comfort. It seemed that Mike and Adrienne were able to carefully listen to each other's ideas and feelings without having to determine whether the other "should" or "should not" feel that way. They each accepted that the other person's perspective, while different, was just as valid as their own. In addition, they were not attempting to determine who was right and who was wrong, so they managed to avoid what might have otherwise become a contentious battle. They seemed genuinely engaged in a collaborative effort to resolve their differences and enjoy a successful social experience with their friends as a result.

Mike said that after the talk, Adrienne hugged him and said, "I feel so much better. I'm really glad we had this talk." What immediately occurred to me upon hearing Mike's comment was that perhaps a primary and fundamental goal of couples whose communication problems are at the core of their troubled relationship should be the ability to have a conversation about emotionally charged issues and come away feeling closer, better, more intimate, and "really glad we had this talk."

IF THERE IS AN US, WHAT HAPPENS TO ME?

Balancing the needs of the individual and the couple…

This intriguing question—in so many variations—has been asked by many people who are struggling with both the joys and the consequences of being involved in a serious romantic partnership. For some, being single is a most desirable state and valued for the many freedoms and opportunities it affords. Many people choose to be single and resist serious romantic involvements because they do not wish to complicate their independent and autonomous lives. For others, being single is a time of waiting; waiting to be partnered so that they can, as one patient remarked, "feel whole again." For them, being single is unacceptable or, worse, a possible indication that they are undesirable, as in "nobody wants me."

Laura, in her mid-fifties, was recently divorced after a ten-year second marriage. She told me that she was enjoying being alone, finding it quite different from the unacceptably lonely existence she envisioned when she first contemplated leaving her husband. Her enjoyment was much more than simply the relief of being out of a conflict-ridden marriage. Her single status was a time of discovery and a cherished opportunity to learn things about herself and about the world around her that she never seemed to have the inclination to do while in the throes of her failing relationship. As a result, Laura has chosen not to become involved with another romantic partner, something she had previously imagined she would find necessary. She told me that she was very busy reestablishing relationships with friends whom she knowingly avoided or even neglected throughout her marriage: "Hal didn't like my friends so I just assumed I could not be with them as long as I was with him." She rediscovered her love of music ("Hal hated music!") and began taking evening courses to help her become more knowledgeable about politics, economics, and art ("Hal hated it when I would go out at night without him and he never wanted to go anywhere so we just stayed home"). As Laura put it, "As long as there was an 'us,' there really wasn't a 'me'."

As you can see, Laura struggled throughout her marriage with what is sometimes referred to as "I and we" conflicts. When she would act in a separate or autonomous way, her husband would accuse her of neglecting him and not adequately investing in the marital relationship. Worried about his occasional threats to leave, Laura would capitulate, having become convinced that it was entirely up to her to save her marriage by making sure Hal was satisfied, even at the cost of her own individual happiness and well-being.

Laura's story is not unique. There are many marital partners—both men and women—who somehow believe that the "us" is much more important, more valuable, more necessary than the "me," and, therefore, live their lives accordingly. What gets lost is the working balance between the needs of the individual and those of the couple. Often, it is not until separation and divorce that they begin to recognize that without a healthy, solid, and well-nourished "I" within the "we," a partnership may feel constricting or, worse, draining in ways that make its long-term success unlikely.

HAVING TO BE RIGHT

How can we learn to attend to the emotional significance of an issue and our partner's point of view?

Some people, it seems, need to be "right" more than they need almost anything else. I am frequently struck by the verbal lengths a person will go when they are very sure of themselves and someone challenges their belief, their memory, or their knowledge about something. This need takes many forms and is an interpersonal transaction often observed in the context of my work with couples.

One of the classic examples occurs when a couple are going somewhere in their car with one partner driving and the other partner navigating or just giving advice about how best to get to their destination. At the proverbial fork in the road, the driver decides to go left while the passenger insists that the other way is the "right" or better way. They get stuck in unanticipated traffic. The nondriving partner becomes angry with the partner who is driving for having chosen the "wrong" way to go and, therefore, causing them to become stuck in traffic. "See, I told you we should have gone the other way," he or she screams at the hapless driver. Rather than share the unfortunate development in a "we're in this together" manner, the nondriver now blames the driver for their plight as though he or she committed a terrible offense. This seems to me to be an example of not only needing to be right, but punishing the other for having managed to be wrong or, in this case, making a reasonable choice that resulted in frustration and disappointment, but did not deserve anger and condemnation.

Before I proceed further, you might find two research reports of interest, given the theme of this essay and the above example chosen to illustrate the issue. In a *USA Today* August 27-28, 2010 report titled "Driving each other nuts," adults who argue with their partner while driving were asked what they argue about. Here are the results:

Calling partner bad driver—31%
Route to take/Asking for directions—36%
Radio/Music Choice—13%
Partner's bad habits in car—11%
Other—9%

Another study found that the average couple can last only twenty-two minutes into a road trip before they get into an argument. The Seat car company from Spain surveyed three thousand people and found that short fuses and long car trips do not mix. The most common cause of automotive acrimony is disputes over directions, with 44 percent of those surveyed saying they argued over which way to go.

In a recent couples therapy session, Marvin wanted to reprocess an argument that he believed typified the kinds of conflicts that he and his wife Jill frequently experience. As he began to describe the specifics of the interaction that had occurred between them, Jill disputed his description of the day, time of day, location, and much of the content of what took place between them. Marvin, evidently having no less a need to be right than Jill, countered by disputing Jill's account of their conflict, which, not surprisingly, created a whole new conflict between them. Fortunately, this occurred in the treatment room where we were able to address it and hopefully help them do better when disputes like these arise in the future.

I often find myself in the position of reminding patients that we are in therapy and not in court, where the facts are much more important and relevant. In therapy, the "court of feelings," we are far more interested in perceptions, emotional triggers, and what past experiences or beliefs are being activated by current interactions with present-day significant others. We are not terribly interested in whether the conflict occurred on Thursday or Friday, in the living room or the kitchen. We don't care whether one person's recall of the specifics is superior to that of their partner. One of the main reasons many couples seem to recycle the same arguments over and over again is because their efforts to resolve conflicts are defeated by their need to be "right" in their retelling, replaying, or reprocessing of a conflict, making it difficult for them to attend to the emotional significance of the issue and the reasons why they are experiencing matters so differently from each other.

AT THE MERCY OF THE OTHER

*We often dread the real or imagined
consequences of provoking emotional
reactions in our partners... . . .*

There are many people who seem to live their lives in a way
that takes the needs, feelings, and vulnerabilities of an important other person into consideration. At first glance, this appears to
reflect caring and sensitivity to that other person; something we
value and consider a necessary requirement for a successful relationship.

The husband who asks himself, "How will my wife feel about
this?" before making a decision that will affect both of them is a
person we admire for his thoughtfulness and his attunement to his
wife's needs and feelings. The adult daughter who wonders about
her father's reaction to her choice of a romantic partner may
appear to be respectful and mindful of her parent's judgment and
ideas about her best interests.

Too often, however, individuals like those in the preceding
examples are not simply interested and concerned about the reactions of important and influential people in their lives. They are
operating with fear or trepidation about the real or imagined consequences of provoking reactions that they feel they must avoid at

all costs. This is what I mean by living "at the mercy of the other."

Dave, a forty-five-year-old business executive, was in a relationship with Eileen, whom he cherished, but with whom he had had a
stormy, volatile relationship for over ten years. In many of his therapy sessions, Dave would discuss his interactions with Eileen in
ways that reflected his fear of offending, upsetting, or provoking
her, making it difficult for him to address his own needs and interests. I would hear comments from Dave such as, "Yes, but Eileen
won't like that," or "I'd love to do that, but I know that Eileen will
refuse." When Dave expressed his desire for a brief, inexpensive
vacation, his wish was immediately followed by, "But Eileen will say
we can't go because it costs too much and we should visit her
mother, instead."

Marsha's story was not very different. "He'll kill me" was an
oft-heard add-on to too many expressions of her wishes and desires
to improve or enhance the quality of her life. It was as though her
dreams, aspirations, plans, and desires had to pass muster with her
husband before they could be allowed to develop any further, let
alone be shared with him and acted upon. She, like Dave, was living at the mercy of an important other person; while understandably wanting to please her partner, she was doing so in a way that
reflected fear and worry, not thoughtfulness and consideration.

Work with these two patients focused on their becoming more
attuned to themselves and better able to act in their own self-inter-
est without fear of consequence if their own needs and desires did
not completely match those of their partners. Neither of these two
people were involved with ogres. Both were helped to understand
and appreciate their own roles in establishing relationships with
their important others that were experienced as or had, in fact,
become oppressive and psychologically limiting. Both patients were

able to improve their relationships once they better established their own autonomy and could think, feel, and plan their lives mindfully, but not fearfully.

HANDLING YOUR NEEDS

Taking responsibility for communicating our decisions and choices...

Recently, I had a telephone interaction with a patient that illustrated a common behavior that can often create difficulties for the individual and those with whom he or she interacts. The patient I refer to is Cathy, the wife in a couple I see for marital therapy. Her husband, Dave, told us that it is difficult for him to understand Cathy's needs because she is so unclear when she communicates them. In addition, rather than stating her desires clearly and directly, she often leaves it up to him to figure out what she needs or assumes that somehow he will understand her needs without her making them evident.

Some people find it difficult to communicate their needs because they are simply uncomfortable having any. Others view "not needing" as some sort of strength and get a self-esteem "boost" by acting as though they need nothing. Some define "not needing" as strength, and view having needs (or, as some refer to it, "being needy") as a weakness. Other people may just not be terribly articulate when it comes to expressing their needs.

Some people prefer not having to express their needs directly, believing that others—certainly their partners—ought to be able to figure out what they need without being told directly. This is viewed by some as an indicator of caring, while not understanding another person's needs may be seen as a sign of not caring.

Cathy needed Dave to bathe their infant son because she was running late. She never asked Dave if he would take care of this task, believing instead that he would observe her lateness and step in to take care of things. When he did not, an argument ensued, with Dave being accused of "insensitivity," being an "out-of-touch" spouse and father, and more. Dave, in his quiet defense, said that he would have been happy to bathe the baby if only he had been asked, since he was unaware of his wife's time problems and was busy caring for another of their children.

Fortunately for the benefit of my work with this couple, I had an opportunity to be on the receiving end of some of Cathy's difficulties expressing her needs. She called me to cancel their next session because of a Halloween event with her son that conflicted with our scheduled time. The exchange between us (along with my observations in hindsight) went something like this:

> Cathy: *"I think I'd like to cancel our session for this week, so that I can go to a Halloween parade with my son. Is that okay?"*

I realized later that Cathy was, essentially, asking my permission to cancel the appointment, rather than declaring her intention to do so.

> Me: *"Well, that's up to you."*

This is the correct response on my part, since I am giving the responsibility for the cancellation back to Cathy, where it belongs.

Cathy: "If you'd rather I not cancel our session, I guess we can just not go to the parade."

Cathy is having a hard time taking responsibility and is now giving authority and responsibility for the decision back to me.

Me: "Well, I'd hate to see that happen, so why don't we meet the following week..."

I blew it! In retrospect, I think I felt put in the position of being the Grinch who would be stealing Halloween from a five-year-old, so I "took the bait" and got Cathy off the hook, rather than asking her a second time: "What would you like to do?"

Clearly, Cathy wanted to cancel the session and so should have done so, rather than tossing the issue over to me for a decision. Fortunately, I saw this, albeit in retrospect, so at least I was able to use my experience with Cathy in a subsequent session in order to help her—and, therefore, the two of them—improve their interactions with each other.

The rules of thumb for handling needs are:

State your needs clearly and directly as the best way to see to it that they get met.

If you are uncomfortable asking for what you need, see what you can do to work that out, so you don't defeat yourself by sending unclear messages to those who have a role in meeting your needs.

Beware a tendency to hand over responsibility to another when certain needs of yours are best met by you.

REACTING AND RESPONDING

The difference between the two and the impact they have on our lives...

The distinction between reacting and responding is an important one and one I have emphasized in my psychotherapy and counseling practice. As far as I am concerned, there is a significant—and, at times, very influential—difference between the two. Responding can be defined as showing a favorable reaction. Reacting, on the other hand, means acting in opposition to a force or influence. Let me illustrate what I believe to be the difference and how it affects us in everyday life.

A reaction may occur within the space of seconds. Since it is usually immediate, it is often without any thought or deliberation, and may, therefore, not be the optimal way in which an individual would have liked or preferred to handle a situation. Reactions are, however, normal and expected. Problems arise when the immediacy of a reaction—as opposed to a response—causes interpersonal difficulties for the reacting individual. Reactions are often emotionally charged and, therefore, tend to be problematic, especially when they may be associated with anger. Those things that we all sometimes say that we wish we could take back are probably reactions, rather than responses.

Responses are typically the outcome of thoughtfulness, reflection, and consideration of the relevant factors, and they are often carefully formulated and well-presented. Responses are not usually those things that we "shoot from the hip," but offer with care, tolerance for differences, and respect for those with whom we interact.

Pamela and Eric have been in couples counseling ten months and are learning to contain their tendency to react, something that has seriously impaired their relationship, and to respond to each other instead. This has not been easy for two individuals with acknowledged difficulties with anger and impulsivity. In a recent counseling session, Pamela told Eric that she would like the two of them to plan a vacation, the first one in over four years. Eric had an explosive reaction to his wife's suggestion: "How can you suggest such a dumb thing when you know we're having financial problems?" He followed this with an emphatic "Absolutely not!" Pamela, not surprisingly, felt attacked and bullied and counterattacked Eric by saying "it's your fault that we are having money problems. If you were a better provider, we could take vacations like our other friends!" Perhaps because of their gains in treatment, both of them were able to stop the exchange before it got any worse, and use the session to examine what had just occurred and to express their regrets at having insulted and hurt each other. Since "react" and "respond" had become part of their emotional vocabulary, Eric apologized to his wife, wished that he had responded rather than reacted, and examined the reasons why he handled Pamela's suggestion the way he did. Pamela wished that she had been able to respond to Eric's provocative reaction by not escalating matters with a provocative reaction of her own.

I had Pamela and Eric "replay the scene," this time demonstrating how they would have liked to respond to each other. This afforded them an opportunity to actually experience a better way of handling matters with each other, rather than just a wish that they had been able to do so the first time around.

When people who are struggling with being too reactive recognize the damage it can do and start to deliberately formulate thoughtful responses, rather than impulsive reactions, their interactions begin to reflect a higher degree of emotional competency. As a result, they live with much less regret and lessen the need to repair the damage to their relationships with others.

DON'T JUST DO SOMETHING— STAND THERE!

Sometimes the most meaningful and effective way to provide help is to be a good listener and not an active problem-solver...

One of the things I have learned in the course of my years providing counseling and psychotherapy is the importance of listening. Some believe "just listening" to be too passive and, therefore, perhaps, not sufficiently helpful. Others appreciate the value and helpfulness of simply having an opportunity to talk about something and feel well-heard and understood by a good listener.

I recall one patient leaving a treatment session and thanking me for "one of the most useful and productive sessions I have ever had." I marveled at the fact that I had been uncommonly silent throughout most of the hour while she spoke intently about an important matter affecting her life. What was clear to me was that she felt listened to and cared for thanks to my undivided attention, even though I had hardly uttered a word.

One of the difficulties that seems to occur in many relationships is that the person listening finds it difficult to accept what they consider to be a passive or inactive role when the other person is expressing upset and appears to need a solution to a troubling problem. A couple I see for marital therapy recently reported an exchange that illustrated this. Carla was expressing upset about her relationship with a brother who had acted offensively toward her. Her husband, Tim, felt as though he had to do something to solve Carla's problem with her brother. Carla had not asked for Tim's help; she just wanted him to listen and be empathic as she shared her feelings. Tim's self-imposed obligation to solve Carla's problem, in the belief that it was his responsibility and an opportunity to prove that he is a good and caring husband, led to marital conflict. He felt inadequate when he could not come up with a solution to Carla's problem. His frustration led to anger at his wife for, as he stated it, "presenting me with a problem I could not solve." Carla felt sandbagged, having never asked for anything more from Tim than empathic understanding and his attentive ear.

What's the message here? Sometimes the most meaningful and effective way to provide help is to be a good listener and not an active problem-solver, especially when that may not have even been asked of you. People often find their own solutions when they have an opportunity to express their feelings in an atmosphere of acceptance, patience, tolerance, and support. Active and attentive silence may, at times, be far more helpful than anything you can say or do to help another.

Thriving

In All of Our Relationships

PROBLEM OR CONDITION?

How can we manage and treat depression?

People who seek out therapists for help with depression and anxiety have often struggled with these feelings on their own for long periods of time. The decision to seek help may come as a result of feeling frustrated and helpless to resolve a particular issue or because of a chronic unhappiness with their lives.

Many people have been living with anxiety or depression for much of their adult lives, if not since childhood. They have had previous therapies that were helpful, enlightening them and contributing information to their quest for self-understanding and improved well-being. Too often, however, patients report that they have acquired a great deal of insight and understanding but have not been able to make some of the changes in their behavior that they originally entered therapy to achieve. One can think of this as being "insight rich and change poor."

One reason for this may be that some people see their difficulties as conditions, rather than problems. Conditions, like diabetes, for example, are not solved, cured, or eliminated. Instead, they are managed and monitored so that they do not get out of hand. Sometimes this may also be true of one's depression or anxiety. It can be chronic and difficult to control, and good management and regulation may be the best that one can do.

However, sometimes it is more helpful to treat anxiety or depression as a problem, not a condition. A problem, by definition, needs to be solved and, therefore, stimulates action. People tend to become more involved in their therapy when they believe that with help, they can do something about their situation. Seeing one's situation as a condition might invite passivity that could undermine the motivation necessary to make desired changes.

Comments from patients like "Well, that's just the way I am," "Nothing I can do about that" or, "I've been this way so long, I'm sure I can't change," often lead to feelings of resignation and defeat. When these beliefs are challenged and reconsidered, a productive therapeutic effort leading to meaningful change is more likely to occur.

Judith, a successful executive in her early forties, was referred by her physician because of his concerns about her chronic anxiety and periodic depression. In her first session, she spoke only of her troubled marriage, saying nothing about the reasons her doctor sent her to me. When I asked her about this, she replied, "Oh that! I'm a very anxious person, and I get really depressed. It gets pretty bad at times, but that's just me."

When she was helped to see how the "condition" she had simply accepted for so many years could benefit from action toward change, she became intrigued, then hopeful, and better able to work toward becoming a much less anxious and depressed individual.

Psychotherapy and counseling are more effective endeavors when someone is actively engaged in the process, believing that change, where possible, is the objective, and that even difficult and chronic emotional states can be aggressively challenged and improved.

THINK BETTER, CHANGE BETTER

*Relieving anxiety by identifying
negative thinking...*

People in psychotherapy or counseling can be helped to see that their problems may be traceable to anxiety-inducing beliefs caused by irrational thought patterns. This awareness can stimulate a productive therapeutic effort leading to meaningful emotional and behavioral change.

The following are some examples of distorted negative thinking that most likely explain why people become anxious or depressed. Recognizing them and taking steps to change them can help regulate one's self-esteem and diminish the frequency and intensity of anxious and depressed states.

Catastrophizing: when you exaggerate the harmful effects or importance of something that happens to you. An example might be the person who receives mild criticism from his boss and becomes certain that he will be fired.

Personalizing: when you see yourself as the cause of a negative event even when there may be no rational basis for doing so. Your child fails a test, and you assume it's because you're a bad parent. Or, when a new and promising romantic partner is not heard from, you conclude that whatever happened must be your fault.

All-or-nothing thinking: the tendency to reduce complex situations to absolutes or to view things in black-or-white terms. This is a common irrational thought pattern that can inspire a depressive state or an episode of anxiety. You know you're not perfect, so you believe that you are a total loser. You have a losing night at the poker table, so you must be the worst poker player in the world.

Overgeneralizing: when you interpret one unpleasant situation as part of an endless pattern. A quite successful and accomplished patient of mine and his wife were outbid on a new house they eagerly wished to own. He concluded that he "never" has any luck at "anything" and is "always" unsuccessful in getting what he wants.

Mental filtering: when someone focuses on the bad while screening out the positive. I once presented a student with an evaluation of her yearlong clinical internship. The report contained numerous and enthusiastic and positive comments along with one mild criticism. After reading the report, her only reaction was "But I don't do that anymore," in reference to the criticism, without any acknowledgment of the extensive praise.

Many patients have been helped by the development of what I refer to as the "third eye" and the "third ear," a means of helping people become more aware of their tendency to engage in some of the irrational thought patterns described above. Essentially, patients observe themselves objectively in order to control reactive behavior. This facilitates their ability to try more rational and positive ways of thinking and feeling on the way to improved self-esteem, as well as less anxiety and depression in their lives.

RELIEF OR CHANGE?

Which is the most meaningful?

Jack, a forty-three-year-old insurance executive, was referred to me by his family doctor for help with his severe panic attacks that had a sudden onset for reasons that were completely unclear to both of them. Jack's symptoms were disabling and resulted in his missing work for several days before his initial appointment with me.

In the first session, I listened to him describe his difficult breathing, chest pains, sleeplessness, and occasional choking episodes, along with his fear of losing complete control and "going crazy." He told me that he had always been an anxious person and had contemplated entering psychotherapy for several years, but never actually did...until now.

The initial consultation with Jack was, in my view, a mixed success. According to Jack, it was "an unbelievable success." We were able to quickly identify the sources of his current anxiety symptoms, which almost immediately provided him with some much-needed relief. We began to outline some of the likely goals of the ongoing therapy he was "very happy to be starting, finally" and for which he eagerly arranged his next appointment with me. As the session wore on, I began to feel concerned that the initial and speedy benefits of this first session might have implications for

Jack's ability to fully engage in the challenging, ongoing work of psychotherapy; something I believed he needed and from which he could derive greater benefit than symptom relief only. I became especially concerned when Jack described his first session as "maybe the best hour of my life!" and described me as "undoubtedly, the best therapist in America!" That's when I thought I probably will never see Jack again.

As it turned out, Jack did attend his second session, and a third, and described the continuing benefits of the work thus far. He was hardly symptomatic, felt "great," no longer thought that he was "losing it," and was wondering whether he really needed therapy after all. Somewhat surprisingly, he asked me to tell him what I thought he should do. In order to help Jack figure this out for himself as much as possible, I did what any therapist worth his stripes would likely do as a first response to such a question: I asked Jack to try to decide independently of my input, so that we could both learn something about his attitudes, thoughts, and feelings, rather than have him simply react to mine. My input followed and consisted of my ideas about the differences between relief and change, with the latter, obviously, being the more ambitious goal and, perhaps, the more durable. I also was mindful, as always, that for some people, relief may be all they want or need. Not everyone wishes to or has the wherewithal to undertake a full course of psychotherapy, especially if they are not in active distress.

After a meaningful conversation about his dilemma, i.e., to stay or to go, Jack decided that he was quite happy with what had occurred and he chose not to pursue further therapy at that time. He asked for and received assurance that my door would always be open and we both acknowledged that we might not ever see each other again. He left describing himself as the "three-session wonder." I later heard from his physician that he was doing quite well, with no further panic attacks. It led me to question whether or not I should revise my thinking to include the fact that sometimes and for some people, relief *is* change and not necessarily something less or less meaningful.

INSIGHT RICH AND CHANGE POOR

*What can we expect as the result
of psychotherapy?*

Many people who see me in order to explore the possibility of doing ongoing psychotherapeutic work together are seeing a psychotherapist for the first time and have little or no understanding about how therapy works, what exactly it is they might expect from the experience, and how to actually get involved in the process. Others have been in therapy before, perhaps many times before, and are, therefore, (as one patient described it) "therapy veterans." They may be seeking help again because of some new development in their lives that warrants additional treatment; or because previous therapeutic ventures, while helpful, did not feel sufficiently complete.

Many patients with previous therapy experience, however, are seeking help again because they remain unhappy with the results of their previous efforts. Patients who feel this way are heard to say things like the following: "I have an excellent understanding of how my various difficulties developed, but nothing much is really any different from when I started my first therapy fifteen or so years ago," "I'm fifty-five now and have become an expert about what's wrong with me, but I'm still the same screwed-up guy I was when I was twenty!" or "I know a lot about myself; I just don't know what to do with it."

The term I use for this problem is: "insight rich and change poor." In fact, when in the initial sessions I have told a new patient that this is what I think they are, the look of recognition—and appreciation—for understanding this is striking!

Psychotherapy or counseling, at best, is a dynamic process that is designed to bring about meaningful change. While the knowledge and insight gained from that process is valuable and a blueprint for change, for most people it is usually not enough to justify the many months and the many dollars often devoted to the therapeutic adventure.

Good counseling or therapy has both therapist and patient keeping a careful eye on the extent to which identifiable and measurable change is taking place. Both need to ensure that the therapy avoids becoming a "research only" enterprise with loads of data, but with little or no evidence of recognizable change.

Change occurs in different ways depending upon the nature of the change being sought, as well as individual styles and efforts made to achieve it. Sometimes change is the result of deliberate and focused effort to bring it about, like breaking a bad habit, trying to rid oneself of a phobia, or overcoming the effects of a trauma. At other times, change may occur unexpectedly—even though it has been worked on—like when one realizes the absence or disappearance of an undesirable behavior or tendency, or a troubled way of thinking.

However change occurs, what is important is that a person looking for substantive change via counseling or psychotherapy emerges from the process feeling as though the hard work and sacrifices made to achieve the changes were well worth the effort and an important gift given to the self for a better, more fulfilling life.

SYNTONIC AND DYSTONIC

How can we be actively engaged in the process of change?

The terms ego-syntonic and ego-dystonic are part of my standard vocabulary as a psychotherapist. I find them extremely useful in my work when evaluating a patient for treatment and I have introduced these terms to patients on many occasions as one way of helping them to better understand themselves.

Ego-syntonic refers to instincts or ideas that are acceptable to the self; that are compatible with one's values and ways of thinking. They are consistent with one's fundamental personality and beliefs. Ego-dystonic refers to thoughts, impulses, and behaviors that are felt to be repugnant, distressing, unacceptable, or inconsistent with one's self-concept.

For a person who is a thief, stealing would be considered ego-syntonic, meaning that it comes naturally, there is unlikely to be any conflict about the act of stealing, and there is little or no guilt, as a result. For most people, stealing would be ego-dystonic, which is probably why we don't do it—and if we did, we would suffer greatly.

One patient, a rather proper and respectable gentleman, began suspecting his wife of having an affair after her frequent explanations for evening absences seemed untruthful. One evening, he decided to check her e-mails while she was out and saw evidence that validated his suspicions. He arrived at his therapy session completely devastated—not by the discovery of his wife's infidelity, but by the fact that he found this out by doing something that "violated my code of ethics and moral standards." Remarkable as it may seem, his own ego-dystonic behavior—invading his wife's privacy by checking her e-mails behind her back—was actually more disturbing to him than the shocking discovery of his wife's betrayal. His emphasis was on figuring out how to best apologize for his transgression and less on how to handle hers.

One of the problems in working with certain psychiatric disorders in a therapeutic setting is the extent to which the disorder is experienced by the patient as ego-syntonic or ego-dystonic. Mental health and medical professionals who work with many eating disorders encounter the problem of patients who believe that their eating behavior is perfectly normal, i.e., ego-syntonic. Anorexia nervosa is just such an example. This is an eating disorder that is characterized by extremely low body weight and body image distortion with an obsessive fear of gaining weight. People who suffer from this condition typically have poor insight and often refuse to accept that their weight is dangerously low, even when it could be deadly. In other words, for the person suffering from this condition, their body and their eating behavior is "normal," or ego-syntonic, in that they feel that there is nothing wrong with how they eat and live.

The task for the professionals involved in treating this disorder is, essentially, to make something that is ego-syntonic for the patient become ego-dystonic instead, so that there might be some leverage to bring about meaningful and necessary emotional, physical, and behavioral change.

Another mental condition is obsessive-compulsive disorder. Obsessions are defined as recurrent and persistent thoughts, impulses, or images that are experienced as intrusive and inappropriate and that cause significant anxiety or distress. Compulsions are repetitive behaviors or mental acts that the person feels driven to perform in response, perhaps, to an obsession. Unlike anorexia nervosa, obsessive-compulsive disorder is ego-dystonic, since the person suffering is fully aware that there is something very wrong with excessive worrying that is not about real-life problems. Similarly, the obsessive-compulsive person knows that something is the matter with behaviors like repetitive handwashing or excessive checking to make sure that the door is locked and the oven is turned off. Despite the strength and persistence of these symptoms, therapy may yield better results since the person suffering recognizes that these symptoms are excessive and unreasonable, i.e., ego-dystonic, and, therefore, may be more able to be actively engaged in the process of change.

TOO LITTLE SLEEP

It's free and available to all, yet we don't always get enough...

Whenever I conduct an initial interview, I ask several questions about a patient's general health, lifestyle choices and habits, and overall physical well-being. These questions are asked also of patients with whom I have an ongoing relationship. This inquiry includes questions about smoking, drinking, drug use, eating behaviors and sleep. With regard to the last of these, I am interested to know whether there is too much (a common sign of possible depression) or too little, and what a person's attitude is toward sleep. Also, I want to know whether there are sleep-related difficulties (e.g., difficulties falling asleep, staying asleep, and waking up) that might need attention.

My impression is that many people are sleeping less than would be considered adequate for optimal overall well-being and functioning. However, the definitions of "too little" vary somewhat and the available research on the subject provides rather mixed information.

The National Sleep Foundation in the United States maintains that seven to nine hours of sleep for adult humans is optimal and that sufficient sleep improves alertness, memory, problem solving ability, and overall health, as well as reducing the risk of accidents. A widely publicized study performed at the University of Pennsylvania School of Medicine demonstrated that cognitive performance declines with fewer than eight hours of sleep. However, a University of California, San Diego study of more than one million adults found that people who live the longest self-report sleeping for six to seven hours each night. It is also true that like so many things, one formula does not necessarily apply to everyone. There are those who thrive well with much less sleep than others who begin to malfunction if they don't satisfy their minimum sleep requirement.

The Centers for Disease Control and Prevention claims that Americans are getting less sleep due to late-night TV watching, Internet surfing, and other distractions. All this sleeplessness can be a nightmare for our mental and physical health, CDC experts caution, calling sleep loss an under-recognized public health problem. What is rarely mentioned in the literature on sleep are the individuals who experience difficulties due to a trauma history associated with their sleeping experiences. One patient reported trouble falling asleep and remaining asleep, and often awakened in a startled state. Her sleep-related difficulties were traceable to an alcoholic father who regularly terrorized the family by coming home drunk and selecting a family member to physically beat from a sleeping to a waking state. Twenty-five years later, this patient reported sleeping to be "unsafe" since she remained "on high alert," having been conditioned to anticipate late-night attacks from her tyrannical and sadistic father. None of this had been presented as a basis for her seeking therapy until her sleep experiences were routinely investigated.

Sleep experts say chronic sleep loss is associated with obesity, diabetes, high blood pressure, stroke, cardiovascular disease, depression, cigarette smoking, and excessive drinking. The CDC said fifty to seventy million Americans suffer from chronic sleep loss and sleep disorders in a country of three hundred million.

The leading researcher of the CDC study, behavioral scientist Lela McKnight-Eily, urged people who often get too little sleep to see a doctor to determine whether lifestyle issues are to blame or whether they might have a sleeping disorder. Also mentioned in the study are two oft-heard common sense recommendations to assist people in their efforts toward better sleep: establish a regular sleep schedule and avoid caffeine or other stimulants before bedtime.

LOCUS OF CONTROL

How do we determine our successes and failures?

There is a concept in psychological literature known as locus of control that is unfamiliar to most people, though once it is defined, it is commonly understood. Locus of control is an individual's belief system regarding the causes of his or her experiences and the factors to which that person attributes success or failure.

Locus of control is usually divided into two categories: internal and external. People with an internal locus of control attribute success to their own efforts and abilities. This may make them more motivated and more likely to learn. People with an external locus of control attribute their success to luck or fate, and will be less likely to make the effort needed to learn. People with an external locus of control are also more likely to experience anxiety since they believe that they are not in control of their lives. This is not to say, however, that an internal locus of control is "good" and an external locus of control is "bad." There are other variables to be considered. However, psychological research has found that people with a more internal locus of control seem to be better off, e.g., they tend to be more achievement-oriented and get better paying jobs.

For several years, I taught a course for mental health professionals who were interested in developing a private practice in psychotherapy. Some, who already had a practice, took the course because they were not doing well and wanted to learn how to be more successful. During the introductory remarks by each student, I was able to mentally divide the class into those having an internal or external locus of control and, therefore, learn a great deal about the class composition. The "internals" said things like "I know it's up to me," "I have to learn how to become more successful," and "I am responsible for what happens in my practice." (Notice the word beginning each statement.) The "externals" were heard to say things like "It's too hard to succeed these days," or "The competition in our field is killing me." The internals clearly believed that it was essentially up to them to succeed. The externals believed that luck, fate, or circumstance were more likely to determine whether or not they became successful than the strength and quality of their own efforts.

Locus of control is often viewed as an inborn personality component. However, there is also evidence that it is shaped by childhood experiences—including children's interactions with their parents. Children who were raised by parents who encouraged their independence and helped them to learn the connection between actions and their consequences tended to have a more well-developed internal locus of control.

The benefits of this were specified in a research study that looked at the potential health effects of the locus of control trait. Researchers found that of more than seventy-five hundred British adults followed since birth, those who had shown an internal locus of control at the age of ten were less likely to be overweight at age thirty, less likely to describe their health as poor, and less likely to show high levels of psychological stress. The major explanation for these findings was that children with a more internal locus of control behave more healthily as adults because they have greater confidence in their ability to influence outcomes through their own actions. They may also have higher self-esteem.

COPING WITH THE EFFECTS
OF TRAUMA

*Not everyone responds to a crisis in the
same way...*

A common and strongly held belief on the part of mental health professionals and others is that everyone needs to express their feelings following a traumatic event in order to recover from its effects. Following the terrorist attacks of September 11, 2001, in New York City, many organizations urged or even required their employees to attend mandatory group sessions in order to help the healing process. Many found sharing their feelings and listening to the feelings of others helpful. Some, however, found talking about the event unhelpful or even harmful to their efforts to process the trauma. Simply put, not everyone copes with the effects of trauma in the same way.

A research study shows that expressing one's thoughts and feelings after a traumatic event is not necessary for long-term emotional and physical health. The study, led by University of California, Irvine psychologist Roxane Cohen Silver, looked at the relationship between immediate expression after the events of 9/11 and mental and physical well-being over time among a nationally representative sample. The research showed, contrary to popular belief, that some people who expressed their thoughts and feelings about the attacks reported increased physical health problems and emotional distress over time. Some participants in the study, who chose not to express thoughts and emotions about the attacks when given an opportunity to do so, appeared to cope successfully and reported fewer diagnosed physical and mental disorders.

On 9/11, 658 employees of Cantor Fitzgerald, a financial services firm that occupied the top floors of One World Trade Center, were killed. I was asked by the American Red Cross of Greater New York to assist the families who had suffered the loss of a loved one on that fateful day. It was clear to me that some family members needed to talk through what had occurred as a way of coping and recovering and were pleased to have an interested mental health professional available to them for that purpose. Others clearly did not desire this form of help, perhaps because they were not ready to express their grief or else had other supports, like family and friends, with whom they could share their thoughts and feelings about the experience. This was also evident weeks later when I called family members to invite them to attend a short-term weekly support group. For some, this was the call they had been waiting for and they eagerly attended the sessions to share and listen to the experiences of others. Others made it clear that the idea of sitting with other sufferers in a group and sharing their grief was likely to cause them greater upset and so they politely declined the offer.

Clearly, it is a myth that everyone must express their distress in order to recover from the effects of trauma. Mandatory or required psychological counseling is often unwarranted and universal intervention is likely to be a waste of resources and, even worse, harmful to some. People who want to talk should do so, but not everyone copes in the same way and it is perfectly healthy not to want to express thoughts and feelings.

HIDDEN DEPRESSION

*Each year, according to the National Institute
of Mental Health, depression strikes fifteen
million Americans . . .*

It is commonly understood in our society that depression is a
disorder of epidemic proportions that too often is unrecognized,
misdiagnosed, and improperly treated. The symptoms can run the
gamut from headaches and chest pains to memory loss and extreme
apathy. Many people with physical symptoms of one kind or
another never realize that their complaints emanate from depression. As a result, many depressed people never bring their problems to medical attention and those who do typically see doctors
who are not specialists in mental health.

According to the findings of a study by the Rand Corporation,
a research institution in Santa Monica, California, the diagnosis of
severe depression is missed at least half the time. The rate of mis-
diagnosis is even higher for the more common milder forms of
depression. Moreover, even when the diagnosis is correct and medication is prescribed, it is frequently the wrong drug or an inadequate dose. Such mistaken treatment, in turn, feeds into the popular
notion that not much can be done about depression, when in fact

at least 80 percent of patients can obtain significant relief through modern antidepressants and psychotherapy.

The problem may be compounded by the fact that the nature of the standard medical office visit does not make vigorous investigation and diagnosis of depression likely. Sometimes patients are asked by their physicians whether or not they are or think they are depressed. Their reply may determine whether the inquiry goes any further and whether a possible diagnosis of depression will be made.

The magnitude of depressive illness in this country dwarfs many other major health problems that receive far more public and professional attention. Each year, according to the National Institute of Mental Health, depression strikes fifteen million Americans. People suffering from depression miss more days of work than those with heart disease. While they are at work, their productivity is often diminished, and at home, their family and other personal relationships can become severely strained.

In its classic forms, depression manifests in feelings of sadness, loneliness, apathy, worthlessness, guilt, pessimism, or hopelessness. Normal drives are severely diminished, resulting in a loss of appetite and sex drive, sleep disturbances, and emotional withdrawal. Memory may be impaired and mental functions and body movements may be slowed. But instead of telling doctors they feel sad or hopeless, at least half of depressed patients complain of a physical problem—headache, constipation, chronic fatigue, weight loss, insomnia, backache, or indigestion—prompting a battery of tests that reveal nothing about the real cause and may result in mistreatment or no treatment at all.

It is important to note that although most people get better on their own within six to twenty-four months without treatment, early diagnosis and treatment can dramatically reduce the length and intensity of the depression. Treatment may also help to reduce the likelihood that the depression will recur. If the depression is severe or if the symptoms interfere seriously with a person's life, antidepressant medication is commonly prescribed, often with positive results.

PATIENT-DOCTOR COMMUNICATION
Learning to talk to our doctors...

have always been curious about an experience often reported by people describing their visits to medical professionals. Understandably, for some, visits to the doctor are anxiety-inducing experiences, especially when there is a need to discuss significant discomfort or an already-diagnosed chronic illness. Many would agree that their very presence in the doctor's office for a medical examination causes some degree of regression and general unease. "White coat syndrome," often resulting in elevated blood pressure readings, is a common experience and something taken for granted by both doctor and patient.

Many people express displeasure with the brevity of their medical appointments and the resulting limited opportunity to discuss their complaints with their physician. Those complaints, frequently, may be more about their emotional issues than their medical condition. For many patients, their doctor is the only one with whom they share personal information of any kind and they may rely on their doctor's response to help them determine the seriousness of their medical or emotional complaints.

Although many physicians naturally listen to their patients with empathy, new studies suggest that too often they are abrupt, apparently uninterested in patients' distress, and prone to controlling the medical interview. All too often, they never find out about serious medical concerns on the minds of their patients. Like any good conversationalist, some of the new research suggests, doctors would do well to listen more and talk less. Dr. Richard Frankel, a sociolinguist at the University of Rochester Medical School, said:

> "The problem is that physicians too readily assume that the patient's first complaint is the most important. But we find that there's no relationship between the order in which patients bring up their concerns, and their medical significance. For most patients we've studied, when their physician gives them the chance to say everything on their mind, their third complaint on average is the most troubling."

Dr. Frankel went on to say that the interviewing habits of many doctors do not allow most patients to get that far.

The research findings suggest that when patients control more of the doctor-patient conversation, being insistent enough to bring up everything on their mind, they often have better medical outcomes. Several years ago, researchers at Tufts University found that a twenty-minute "coaching session" for patients while they waited for their physicians had positive health effects. Those with hypertension and ulcers, as well as a group with diabetes, fared better than the noncoached patients. In the coaching sessions, patients were helped to determine their agendas and offered techniques for overcoming embarrassment, anxiety, or timidity in talking with the doctor. Research findings revealed that the coached patients were much more effective in both giving and getting information in their communication with their doctor. Coached patients with hypertension had systolic blood pressure readings 15 percent below their earlier readings, while those with diabetes had 12 percent lower blood glucose readings. These findings suggest that the more assertive the patient is, the more likely he or she is to feel heard and understood, fare better medically, and come away with a better understanding of the information given by the doctor.

HINDSIGHT, INSIGHT, AND FORESIGHT

Change means different things to different people...

As a clinical social work psychotherapist, I am often asked a few very understandable and meaningful questions by patients: "How exactly do people change?" "How will I know when I am really different?" Questions like these provide an excellent opportunity to clarify the objectives of the treatment. This helps both clinician and patient keep a sharp eye on the process so that the goal of eventual change is not lost.

Frequently, counseling and psychotherapy patients express that after extensive treatment, they feel much more knowledgeable about their difficulties and have achieved a richer understanding of how and why their issues developed. However, they do not feel that they have made significant changes. I call this frequently seen condition being "insight rich and change poor."

One of the ways I discuss change with my patients is by defining three states of awareness: hindsight, insight, and foresight. In the process of trying to change, hindsight is often the first way in which a person becomes more self-aware. Looking back at a problematic choice or action provides a useful beginning in the effort to function differently. "Gee, I wish I had not done that" or "I can't believe I did the same dumb thing again" are examples of hindsight that offer an opportunity to pay closer attention and work on problematic behaviors.

Insight can occur when a person becomes self-aware during the commission of a regrettable action or behavior. "There I go again" is a phrase that often accompanies an insightful moment. The advantage of insight over hindsight is that insight may occur in time for a regrettable action or decision to be avoided. Hindsight, by definition, is always after the fact.

The final goal in promoting change is achieving the state of self-awareness, or foresight. Change may be best achieved when someone can look over the horizon and foresee an opportunity or situation where they can employ their hindsight and insight and function in a way compatible with their therapeutic goals. This might be the operational definition of meaningful change. Let me illustrate with a brief patient example.

Laura, a married woman with two young children, wanted to change the "terrible" way she related to her aging, "difficult-to-tolerate" widowed mother. During the hindsight phase of her treatment, Laura's regret at how she behaved between sessions dominated the conversations as we tried to understand and modify her behavior. In phase two, her capacity for insight enabled her to be more reflective and better able to handle her anger and resentment, resulting in much less regret and decreasing further damage to her self-esteem and her relationship with her mother. In the third phase, her foresight, along with many other treatment gains, enabled her to anticipate the visits with a better sense of emotional control and determination to conduct herself differently.

Change means different things to different people. In therapy and in life, it's important that we always see change as possible and work with determination to achieve our goals.

Resources

According to the National Institute of Mental Health (NIMH), the approximate number of Americans who experiencea mental health disorder in a given year is 61,500,000. That's one in four adults. The estimated economic cost of untreated mental illness in the U.S. is $100,000,000,000. This includes unemployment, unnecessary disability, substance abuse and more. It is quite meaningful to note that the percentage of individuals with mental illness who saw improvement in their symptoms and quality of life after participating in some form of treatment was 70-90%. Another noteworthy statistic is that the percentage of adults who did not receive mental health treatment in 2012 was 60%.

I have always been concerned about the many people who need and would likely benefit from mental health services, but manage not to seek appropriate help. There are many reasons for this. Among them are unfamiliarity with existing resources and how to find them, fear of the unknown, myths and misperceptions about what happens in counseling or psychotherapy, and many more. There are both true and untrue stories about the experiences of those who have received help that often serve as a disincentive to those in need and who might benefit. Like so many who do not seek required medical attention for fear of learning that something is terribly wrong with them physically, so do many not get help for depression, posttraumatic stress, anxiety disorders, for example, and remain suffering unnecessarily sometimes for many years or even throughout their entire lives.

If any of the ideas or concepts discussed in these essays interests you and you would like additional information, or if you or someone you know has a mental health problem, there are ways to get more information and help. Use these resources to find help for you, a friend, or a family member.

Please note that these resources are provided for informational purposes only. The list is not comprehensive and does not constitute an endorsement by me.

For general information on mental health and to locate treatment services in your area, call the Substance Abuse and Mental Health Services Administration (SAMHSA) Treatment Referral Helpline at 1-88-662-HELP (4357). SAMHSA also has a Behavioral Health Treatment Locator on its website that can be searched by location.

National agencies and advocacy and professional organizations have information on finding a mental health professional and sometimes practitioner locators on their websites. Examples include but are not limited to:

Anxiety and Depression Association of America
Depression and Bipolar Support Alliance
Mental Health America
National Alliance on Mental Illness

University or medical school-affiliated programs may offer treatment options. Search on the website of local university health centers for their psychiatry or psychology departments.

You can also go to the website of your state or county government and search for the health services department.

If you have any interest in obtaining counseling or psychotherapy for yourself or need a referral for mental health services for someone in your life, I would be happy to assist you to find the help you need whatever your location. I can be reached by e-mail at rbjoelson@aol.com or by telephone at 212 369-1239.

Acknowledgments

It is heartwarming to realize how many people have been crucial to the successful completion of this book.

The thoughtful and astute insights and observations, the careful and creative guidance, and the enthusiastic support of my two editors, John Niernberger and Alice Peck, have been personally and professionally invaluable. I am very grateful to them along with Duane Stapp for making the development of this book such an interesting and joyful enterprise. Arlene McBride, librarian and researcher par excellence, and Laine Cohen, with her sharp and critical eye, helped to organize and tighten up the essays and thus make them better. Their tireless work during a family vacation meant a great deal to me and I thank them with all my heart. The cheerleading of Matthew Joelson, Andrew Joelson, Todd Cohen, and Jenn Ahn from the sidelines has meant the world to me and I thank them all. My gratitude to Rosalind Cohen for her infinite patience, consistent encouragement, and pride in my achievements has always enabled me to move ahead with confidence and freedom in this and many other ventures. My gratitude for her unending gifts knows no bounds.

I am grateful to the editors of *The New York Resident* for publishing twelve of my essays in the health column of their newspaper and by requiring my submissions to be five hundred words or less forcing me to happily learn the art of conveying as much information as possible in very few words.

A special acknowledgment is due to Joanna Griffith who, from the very beginning, supported my literary endeavors and helped me find ways to bring them into the world.

My patients, to whom this book is dedicated, have certainly added immeasurably to the quality of my thinking and my writing. They provided the material for the essays and then, I believe, benefitted from the development of my ideas and ability to employ them in the psychotherapeutic treatment experience. My appreciation for all of them is enormous.

CPSIA information can be obtained
at www.ICGtesting.com
Printed in the USA
BVOW08s0231281016
466290BV00001B/41/P